Kitchen Secrets *of the* Vinegar Ladies

by

Dixie Anderson
Tami Feulner

SILVERLEAF
PRESS

Acknowledgements

This book would not be complete if we didn't take a moment to express sincere thanks and deep appreciation to those special people behind the scenes who have helped make this happen. First, to our husbands, the guys who believed in us, even when we didn't believe in ourselves. Thank you for your endless support mentally, emotionally and physically. There aren't many men who will claim that his wife is "sour" and be proud of it! To our kids, the taste-testers of our experiments, thanks for being willing subjects and good sports even if the smell in the house made you want to run and hide. To our special ladies, "the Vinaigrettes," thank you for your very special friendship. The relationships we share will be held dear to our hearts forever. And to our moms, Barbara and Barbara. Without their inspiring example as women, moms and cooks, we would not be what we are today. Thanks moms! And finally thanks to all our "vinegar friends" who have shared ideas, recipes and especially enthusiasm. You have helped to make this a chapter in our lives that we will never forget!

Silverleaf Press Books are available exclusively through Independent Publishers Group.

For details write or telephone
Independent Publishers Group, 814 North Franklin St.
Chicago, IL 60610, (312) 337-0747

Silverleaf Press
8160 South Highland Drive
Sandy, Utah 84093

Table of Contents

Introduction

Do you believe in destiny? Do you believe things happen for a reason? There we were, two stay-at-home moms flying along by the seat of our pants. What with husbands, kids, dogs, mortgages, car pools to drive, laundry to wash, and toilets to clean, who would have known that answering a knock at the front door and a little trip to Boston would change the course of existence as we knew it.

It all began when a neighbor came by to share the bounty of her herb garden. As she extended her hand, we fully expected to see a zucchini squash. Instead, she held up a jar containing a clear liquid with 4 or 5 pink blossoms floating on top. She explained that her chives were blossoming, so she had made us some chive blossom vinegar. "Just let the chives flavor the vinegar for a couple of weeks," she told us, "remove the blossoms, and you will have a lovely light pink vinegar that will be ready to drizzle over freshly steamed vegetables." "It is delicious!" she exclaimed with such enthusiasm that we could not help but be intrigued. Over the next few days we let this idea of flavored vinegar marinate in our minds. If vinegar could be flavored with chive blossoms, what other flavors could be infused into this smelly fermentation? A short time later, a trip to Boston would further tantalize our taste buds as a visit to the cranberry bogs unveiled the most beautiful bottle of cranberry flavored vinegar we had ever seen.

It was about this time that we were asked to teach a craft class for a women's group. "Maybe something on flower arranging," they suggested. But alas, our minds were busily percolating with visions of flavored vinegars dancing in our heads. "No thank you," we politely declined. "However, we do have an idea!"

In retrospect, if we had been able to look into a crystal ball and seen the tidal wave that was about to hit, we would have run for our lives. But we did not. Instead, we soon found ourselves being consumed. And once our creative juices started to flow, we were unstoppable. We would even wake in the middle of the night with a new idea and could hardly wait until morning to try it. It must have been a comical sight as we shoved everything we could think of into a bottle and poured vinegar over it to see what would happen. It wasn't long before we had what is now known as "The Fabulous Five"—Provencal, Hot Pepper, Garden Blend, Tangy Citrus and Lemon Dill. These are the staple vinegars—the ones that are a must in your pantry. It's kind of like a black skirt and a white blouse; they're an essential part of every good wardrobe.

With our vinegars looking lovely and the kids at school, we got all dressed up one day and took our show on the road. We thought maybe, just maybe, we could sell our beautiful bottles of vinegar to a retail store. When a very prominent local merchant agreed to sell our product, we were delighted. But it was when they asked us to come and teach classes on how to cook with the flavored vinegars that we nearly fell off our chairs. Up to that point, we had merely whisked together a few lovely vinaigrettes. Now the pressure was really on!

Our families like to tease us that what happened next has caused them to seek professional counseling—they became our guinea pigs and our kitchens were transformed into test labs. Any of our kids will tell you, it is not a good day when your friends tell you that you smell like vinegar. But that is what happened. Indeed, we were all becoming a little pickled. Truthfully, being pressured to cook with the vinegars was actually a blessing for us. Otherwise, we may have never fully exposed flavored vinegar in all of its fragrant glory.

Within a very short time, the phone began to ring. Classes were scheduled and we soon found ourselves teaching groups about flavored vinegar 3 or 4 times each week. Up to this point, we had called our business "Flavors," but as we would receive phone calls, the women would ask, "Is this the vinegar ladies?" We soon realized that it was a simple and unmistakable title. And so we were born again as…"The Vinegar Ladies."

To toot our own fermented horn, we were simply an overnight vinegar sensation! We found ourselves staying up all night to prepare ingredients for the next day's classes. We hired many of our stay-at-home mom friends to prepare packets. Later, when we were forced to schedule multiple classes on the same day, we sent them out as presenters. To this day, we affectionately refer to them as our "Vinaigrettes." No sweeter women will there ever be. We are sure that there were times when they would purposely avoid direct eye contact because they were afraid we would ask them to chop veggies or wash bottles. But they never let us down. Thanks ladies!

It really was a mind blower. To think that one day we were just your average stay-at-home moms and the next, we were "celebrities"—albeit on a somewhat sour level. It didn't matter if we were at the mall, the grocery store or even the theatre to take in a new movie, we were constantly stopped and asked, "Aren't you the Vinegar Ladies?" We reluctantly autographed recipe books—that just seemed too weird…no one had ever wanted our signatures except for an occasional request by our kids to sign a permission slip to go on a field trip. Yes…it was getting a little out of hand.

It was a good thing that we had lived in the same homes for years and our neighbors knew us well. Otherwise, they may have been suspicious of the kind of activity that was no longer occasional, but rather very constant. Large trucks made regular deliveries. Suburbans and Minivans would pull up to our garages each evening, load up with ice chests and boxes, only to return late that night with nothing but a money bag. And there was the constant stream of women—who were completely vinegarized—coming to our homes to buy bottles and other assorted supplies. Thank heaven our husbands were very supportive, because they no longer were allowed to park in the garage…because now it was "Vinegar Central." We would lift the garage door and the store was "OPEN." We finally had to set regular hours because our telephones and doorbells would ring from 6:00am until 10 or 11:00 pm. We were weary yet exhilarated at the same time.

And although there may have been times when they would have questioned it, we never really forgot our families. The overflowing laundry basket and pile of dirty dishes kept us grounded. Truthfully, we couldn't have done it all without them and their constant support. And thank heaven for the many funny moments that kept us laughing…like the time a truck driver who was delivering a pallet full of glass bottles, dumped them off the tailgate of the truck and all of a sudden instead of 1,500 bottles, we merely had a very large pile of broken glass. We'll never forget the look on that young man's face. Or when Tami would surprise the women during a class and take a swig of vinegar right out of the bottle. This would always create a stir.

Christmas was approaching and hundreds of women were demanding more than we could give. So we did the only thing we could under the circumstances. We put on an extravaganza, a full-on affair…The Vinegar Affair! What's the Vinegar Affair? Imagine, if you can, a hotel exhibition room filled with 1,000 or so vinegar-crazed women, pallet after pallet of vinegar, 30 or 40 cases of fruits and vegetables, 80 pounds (36kg) of fresh herbs, 2,000 or so decorative bottles, 12 lovely lady Vinaigrettes, 2 buff vinegar men (our husbands, the muscle behind the beauty), and 2 totally insane Vinegar Ladies. Take our word for it, it was WILD. After that, we had an affair every six months, whether we needed it or not.

Well, it was a wild ride. Now, ten years later…what are we doing? We're still making and cooking with flavored vinegar. And now you have taken the first step in joining us on our journey by purchasing this book. In all honesty, we must make this disclaimer…we are not gourmet cooks! We have never attended culinary school or received a degree in nutrition. We are simply wives and moms who are always looking for new and healthy ideas to incorporate into our cooking. It will become obvious in no time at all that we are far from serious. We enjoy one another's sense of humor, even if no one else does. And what better way to discover something new than to be with your best friend, working 80-hour weeks and having fun while you're doing it?

Anyway, we know you'll enjoy making and using our flavored vinegars. Let your imagination run wild. We did. And now they call us…The Vinegar Ladies!

Vinegar Basics

F lavored vinegars are beautiful, both as a decorative touch to your kitchen counters and as a staple in every-day cooking. They can also make wonderful gifts for friends and neighbors. It seems like the local grocery stores are carrying more and more flavors of vinegar to choose from, but what we want to stress is how fun and easy flavored vinegars are to make at home. The ones you make yourself are fresher, more flavorful, and each is unique. The price difference is nice, too.

Upon looking at our recipes, you will see just how easy it is to make flavored vinegars. The trick is to trust yourself. We have taught hundreds of classes to thousands of ladies (and some gentlemen), and with very little help from us, they have made gorgeous bottles of vinegar in hardly any time at all. We could say that making beautiful vinegars is a skill that must be learned through years of practice. But to our delight, we can report that we quickly learned that it required absolutely no artistic ability. Anyone with a funnel and a long wooden skewer can make beautiful flavored vinegars. Upon completion of each new creation, you will want to stand back, wave your hands like Vanna White, and exclaim a triumphant "Tah Dah"!

In this section, our goal is to help you understand a little bit about vinegar. With a title like "The Vinegar Ladies," we are often approached with questions regarding this smelly liquid. Let us try to put your mind at ease.

What is vinegar and where does it come from?

Does it contain alcohol?

In very basic terms, vinegar comes from any liquid that contains enough sugar to support an alcoholic fermentation. So basically, sweet juice that will ferment. The word "vinegar" comes from the French "vin" (meaning "wine") and "aigre" (meaning "sour"). So there you have it, "sour wine." For centuries, people in countries all over the world have made their own vinegar. They used the staple product of their region as their main ingredient. Apple cider vinegar comes from the United States, rice vinegar from China and Japan, wine vinegar from France and Spain, and so on.

So, we'll give you a little example of how apple cider vinegar was first discovered. Someone made some wonderful apple juice and stored it in a wooden keg. The keg was forgotten. The apple juice, having natural sugar, and time on its hands, started to ferment. Thus it became alcoholic. The real apple cider. (At this point, someone discovered this fermented brew and liked it. But now we're going off on a tangent, so back to the forgotten keg of apple cider.) The air brought a bacteria to the alcoholic apple cider that is known as "the mother." We have thought many times that this was a terrible choice of names for a bacteria that makes vinegar. But anyway, "the mother" turns the cider into vinegar. The bacteria in the cider is whitish in color and not very appealing. At this point, whoever drew the short straw had to take a sip of the rotting cider and—*voila*!—discovered the wonders of vinegar. The cider vinegar contains no alcohol. None whatsoever! The "mother" took care of that, as most good mothers always will. Now, of course, this process takes a lot longer than we all have time for with our busy, hectic lives. So, in the next couples of paragraphs we'll talk about the types of vinegars that are available to buy so that you can choose a vinegar to use as the base in your flavored vinegars. And that is what this book is all about it!

It is important to note that different types of vinegar vary in the degree of acidity. The higher the acetic acid level the stronger the vinegar. Government regulations state that a liquid must be 4% acetic acid in order to be called vinegar. Always check the label for the exact percentage. American vinegars are usually 5%. Wine vinegars are usually 6%. Rice vinegar is one of the mildest at just slightly above 4%.

The Basic Five:

Balsamic Vinegar

We don't use this as a base vinegar because of its strength and extremely dark color. We do, however, love the rich, aromatic flavor and highly recommend always having a bottle in your pantry. We suggest spending the money on a good quality Italian balsamic; the older the better (and unfortunately, the pricier).

Red and White Wine Vinegar

Soon you will realize that these are our favorite base vinegars. They are beautiful in color, delicate in flavor and can be purchased at an affordable price. Whether you are using herbs or fruits, they will not overpower your flavorings. They create a nice combination.

Apple Cider Vinegar

Although we like the amber color of this vinegar, it can be overpowering when used as a flavored vinegar base. However, small quantities always add an extra punch to your recipe.

Seasoned Rice Vinegar

Very delicate and so so good, you'll want to swig it straight out of the bottle. We prefer the seasoned rice vinegar over the plain rice vinegar because of the added sweetness. You can, however, purchase it both ways and make your own decision. We are especially fond of this vinegar combined with hot peppers. It makes a really fun combination.

Other Popular Vinegars:

Sherry Vinegar

Brown in color and slightly sweet to the taste. We suggest sprinkling it directly on mixed greens along with a flavored oil. Probably not one to use in flavored vinegars as it is not very pretty and has a extremely strong flavor.

Champagne Vinegar

As to be expected, this vinegar is very expensive. It has a delicate taste and is very refined. The pale gold color is quite stunning. We think it would make a wonderful base vinegar if it weren't so darned expensive.

Malt Vinegar

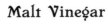

We feel that this vinegar is suitable as a condiment and not much else. Strong in flavor and dark in color, it is very undesirable for flavored vinegar. We do, however, love it with our fish and chips!

Distilled Vinegar

A clear vinegar, made from diluted, distilled alcohol. Do you really want to put a distilled alcohol by-product in your food? We didn't think so. But it works wonders in many other household tasks. Refer to our section called, "The Little Treasure."

A Few Final Notes

Vinegar is best stored in glass bottles. Never store in canning jars with metal lids as the vinegar will corrode the metal and develop a nasty flavor. We have found that corks are best for airtight closure. Whenever you are heating vinegar, be sure to use a stainless steel pot. Vinegar will corrode aluminum and other metals and will not only ruin your vinegar, but your pan as well. And finally, it is best to store vinegar out of direct sunlight. Although the bottles may look beautiful on your windowsill, they may develop a cloudy, undesirable appearance (while it's still okay to use, it's not very pretty to look at).

Flavored Vinegars

 To amend a well-known line from Walt Disney, we invite you: "Welcome to the Wonderful World of Vinegar." It truly is the happiest place on earth. And is completely legal, although our husbands may say it can become an addiction.

The possibilities of different flavored vinegars are limited only by your imagination. On the following pages we have selected some of our most prized creations. Our babies! However, this is not to say that we didn't have some real stinkers as well. We would encourage you to be brave and stretch your creative juices…small quantities at a time. Remember that sometimes too much of a good thing is not so good.

The first thing that you will want to do is purchase your base vinegars (i.e., red and white wine vinegar and seasoned rice vinegar). The most economical way to do this is to purchase it by the gallon. We recommend trying your local price club first. We have found this to be our most valuable resource. If they don't currently carry these vinegars, be sure to place a request for them. As a last resort, you can always find them in the vinegar section of your local market. However, they will be in much smaller bottles and more expensive.

Now, let's talk bottles. To make the recipes easy to understand, we have scaled them to fit one 17-ounce bottle. The only exception to this would be our berry vinegars, which are prepared in large quantities on the stove. In your world, you can use any size or shape of glass bottle you choose (make sure they are washed thoroughly). Simply adjust the ingredient list to accommodate your bottle. It is best if the bottle can be corked securely. In recent years, decorative bottles have become very popular and are readily available. Empty wine bottles can also be washed and reused to store your favorite vinegars. Corks of just about every size can be found at most local hardware and craft stores. For a nice, professional touch, shrink-wrap seals of various colors can be purchased over the internet. To shrink these seals onto your corked bottle, simply apply heat from a hairdryer or heat gun.

Dehydrating and Preparing to Bottle

If there is one trick to making flavored vinegars, dehydrating is probably the granddaddy of them all. It is not a difficult task, simply one that takes a little time and "know how" to do well. If you try to eliminate this step, when called for, you will cause yourself great frustration and will most likely sacrifice lovely looking bottles of vinegar.

First: Wash thoroughly the fruit that is to be dehydrated, removing all produce stickers, etc.

Second: Slice the fruit. The best way to do this is with a slicer, electric or manual. The desire is to have fruit slices that are approximately ⅛ inch thick. If they are too thin, the meat of the fruit will fall apart. If they are too thick, you won't be able to roll them small enough to get them into the bottle.

Third: Now you are ready to dehydrate! You will need to buy or borrow an electric food dehydrator that blows warm air. Place the sliced fruit on the trays and place in the dehydrator. With the temperature set at the high setting, turn on and let dehydrate for approximately 30 minutes. The dehydrating time may vary so this is not the time to move away from the kitchen. The desired goal is to be able to gently roll the fruit slices without breaking the rind or the meat of the fruit. Apples usually take a little longer. You will notice that the pieces will become more pliable as they dry. If the fruit becomes hard and brittle, you have gone way too far. Once you have your fruit at the right pliability, place the slices in a Ziploc bag. This will keep them perfectly until you're ready for them.

Fourth: Follow the recipe instructions to create your beautiful bottles of vinegar.

Well, that about does it for Vinegar 101. Please don't stress! This truly is one of the easiest and most satisfying of all hobbies. It is very difficult to mess this up. In hundreds of classes with literally thousands of women who have made our vinegars (and many would admit that they didn't have an artistic bone in their body), each bottle is unique and simply beautiful.

Apple Cinnamon Vinegar

This beautiful, autumn vinegar combines the best of the fall harvest to create a vinegar with an aroma that will remind you of Mom's homemade apple pie. From baked apples to taffy to a sweet apple vinaigrette, you will find an endless list of uses for this delightful vinegar.

6-inch (15cm) cinnamon stick
6 or 7 apple slices (very thin and slightly dehydrated for flexibility—see instructions on page 16)
2 tsp. whole cloves
2 Tbs. whole allspice
16oz. (455g) white wine vinegar
lemon juice

Place allspice, cloves and cinnamon stick in glass bottle. Place the apple slices in the lemon juice for 30 seconds to keep from discoloring prior to dehydrating. Follow dehydrating instructions of page 16. Once apples have been prepared, arrange them to your satisfaction in the bottle. You can use a long wooden skewer to help place them attractively. Pour the vinegar over your ingredients. Cork and store in a cool place. Vinegar will be infused and ready to use in approximately 10 days.

Note: When selecting your apples, it is best to choose an apple that is non-waxed. The vinegar causes the wax on the apple skin to turn white and flake off into your vinegar. It won't hurt the flavor of the vinegar, but it doesn't look very appetizing. If in doubt, ask your grocer for non-waxed apples. Makes 1 bottle.

Basic Berry Vinegar

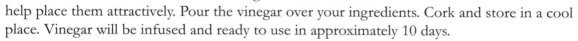

Berry vinegars are beautiful and a must-have in any vinegar lover's collection. They take a little longer to make, so we suggest making larger quantities at one time. The best time to do this is when the berries are in season and can be found at an affordable price. Your friends will love to receive a bottle of your berry vinegar as a gift. Some of our favorites are strawberry, raspberry, blueberry, and blackberry.

1 gallon (4L) red wine vinegar
4 pints (2L) of berries
2 cups sugar (optional)
large coffee filters

In a large stainless steel pot, combine vinegar, berries and sugar and bring to a simmer on medium heat. (Never let the vinegar boil!) Let simmer for 30 minutes. Remove from heat and let sit covered overnight. The next day, place coffee filter inside of a large colander and place colander over a large bowl or pot. Pour vinegar into the filter very slowly. You may need to change filter if it becomes slow. The end product should be beautifully clear and free of any pulp. Pour into bottles and cork. It is now ready to use in any of your favorite recipes.

Note: Many people ask why we don't leave any fruit in the vinegar. The answer is completely aesthetic. Berries tend to loose their color in vinegar. Over time they go a terrible gray color and look very unappetizing. By infusing them into your vinegar and then removing them, your vinegar will stay beautiful indefinitely. Makes several bottles.

Basic Herb Vinegar

Vinegar flavored with herbs is hardly a new idea. However, commercial herb vinegar often lacks flavor. If you are like us, our gardens are often overflowing with herbs. The question is always "What do I do with it all?" Use the bounty to make wonderfully flavored vinegar. It is quick and simple to make and will produce a delightful result.

16oz. (455g) vinegar of your choice (we prefer a wine vinegar for its mild flavor)
1-2 cups fresh herbs (keep it simple with one variety or make a lovely bouquet by combining several different types of herbs)
2 tsp. peppercorns
2-3 peeled garlic cloves

Place desired herbs, garlic and peppercorns in pre-washed glass bottle. Pour vinegar into the bottle over the ingredients. Cork tightly and let stand for 10 days to allow flavors to infuse into the vinegar. Makes one 16oz. (455g) bottle.

Note: Combining herbs with other ingredients can make a variety of fun and delightful vinegars. Adding things like lemon peel, orange peel, celery seed, poppy seeds, even cinnamon sticks can really bring out your creative juices.

Chive Blossom Vinegar
(and other onion variations)

These vinegars are terrific to have on hand to add an extra punch of flavor to almost anything non-sweet that you are cooking. The chive blossom is a sentimental favorite as it was one of our first introductions to flavored vinegars. It is great drizzled straight from the bottle onto freshly steamed summer vegetables. Adds a quick shot of pungency to Caesar salad dressing, mayonnaise, marinades and vinaigrettes. Although a little strong, we are sure you will find a favorite recipe to use them in.

16oz. (455g) white wine vinegar
6-8 chive blossoms, shallots or other desired variation

Simply place desired ingredients in bottle. Top with the vinegar and cork tightly. Wait approximately 10 days before using. Makes 1 bottle.

Cranberry Cinnamon Vinegar

This makes a beautiful ruby-red colored vinegar and is especially festive during the holiday season. You will find a number of recipes in this book that use this vinegar. This is a great gift for those names on your Christmas list that are hard to buy for. Brimming with fresh cranberry flavor, this pleasantly tart and spicy vinegar adds pizzazz to salads, sauces and marinades.

6-inch (15cm) cinnamon stick (per bottle)
6 cups fresh cranberries
1 gallon (4L) red wine vinegar
2 cups sugar
large coffee filters

In a colander, rinse cranberries with cold water and drain well. In a stainless steel pot, bring the cranberries, vinegar and sugar to a simmer. DO NOT BOIL! Simmer gently, uncovered for approximately 30 minutes. Turn off heat, cover and let stand overnight.

Place one large coffee filter inside a colander over

a large bowl. Pour cranberry mixture slowly through the coffee filter. The cranberry vinegar will be clear and sparkling. Discard cooked cranberries. In each empty bottle, place a cinnamon stick and ½ cup or so of rinsed, fresh cranberries. Pour infused vinegar into each bottle and cork tightly. Allow to sit for about a week for the cinnamon flavor to infuse. Enjoy! Makes several bottles.

Creamsicle Vinegar

We are not trying to be funny with this name; it's just that a creamsicle is exactly what this vinegar smells like. So if you love that orange/vanilla taste, your saliva glands will be working overtime when you get a whiff of this fun vinegar. Terrific as a vinaigrette over salad greens or as a sauce over fruit. And need we say it looks beautiful just sitting there on your counter as well?

> 16oz. (455g) white wine vinegar
> 8 thin slices of orange (slightly dehydrated—see instructions on page 16)
> 1 vanilla bean

After dehydrating orange slices, place them into your bottle along with the vanilla bean. Pour vinegar over ingredients and cork tightly. Your vinegar will be infused in approximately 10 days. Makes 1 bottle.

Farmers Market Vinegar

Nothing makes us happier than to visit a farmers market on a Saturday morning. Maybe that's saying a little too much about our personalities. Anyway, everything looks so healthy and appealing. In fact, we get a lot of our ideas just roaming up and down the aisles. There are always vegetables that we have never seen before for sale that intrigue us and give us inspiration. And with that we'll introduce you to Farmers Market Vinegar. It is closely related to Garden Blend Vinegar, but it has a slightly hot flavor along with a tart kick. It will remind you of the booths at the market. We're sure you've got a lot of vegetable recipes to try this in. Good Luck!

2 asparagus spears
2 green onions
5 baby carrots (peeled)
6 Thai chili peppers (red)
2 fresh bay leaves
2 tsp. Mustard seeds
2 tsp. whole peppercorns
3 sprigs fresh rosemary
2-3 cloves fresh garlic (peeled)
16oz. (455g) white wine vinegar

Gently wash all herbs and vegetables. Place rosemary, asparagus and green onion in a tall bottle. Add carrots, peppers, bay leaves, mustard seeds, garlic and peppercorns. Pour white wine vinegar over the ingredients. Cork tightly. Allow 10 days for the ingredients to infuse their flavors into the vinegar. Makes 1 bottle.

Garden Blend Vinegar

This wonderful concoction's aroma is so tantalizing that you'll have to stop yourself from drinking it straight from the bottle. And the flavors are so distinctive you'll have no trouble using this vinegar in a variety of dishes—vinaigrettes, vegetable marinades, potato salads, veggie dips. You're only limited by your imagination. Just a splash can do marvelous things.

16oz. (455g) white wine vinegar
2 or 3 long, thin slices of carrot
1 asparagus spear
1 long, thin slice of celery
2 pea pods
2 green beans
1 long thin slice of green pepper
1 long thin slice of red pepper
2 cloves garlic (peeled)
1 sprig parsley
2 green olives
2 tsp. whole peppercorns

Place all ingredients in your bottle. Longer items should go in first. This will allow the small items to fill in the empty spaces. Pour vinegar in to fill. Cork tightly and let infuse for approximately 10 days before using. Makes 1 bottle.

Herbed Pomegranate Vinegar

Well, you're just going to have to make this vinegar. It's too pretty and yummy not to! We also have several recipes that call for it. Most of them are holiday creations that are great for entertaining. This recipe makes several bottles, so why not give them away for special gifts. Nobody will ever believe you made them yourself.

1 gallon (4L) red wine vinegar
12 pomegranates (quartered and quartered again)
2 cups sugar
16 sprigs fresh rosemary
several large coffee filters

Combine the pomegranates, sugar, and the vinegar in a stainless steel pot. Heat to simmer on your stove, stirring frequently. Do not let the mixture come to a boil. Let the mixture simmer for 30 minutes. Take the pot off the heat, cover, and let stand overnight. The next day place a coffee filter into a large colander over a large, clean pot. Strain the vinegar mixture through the coffee filter and into the pot. You should have a beautiful, crystal clear vinegar. Place gently washed rosemary sprigs into several bottles with 3 or 4 per bottle. Pour the vinegar over the rosemary. Cork tightly. Allow 1 week for the rosemary to infuse into the pomegranate vinegar. Makes several bottles (depending on their size).

Hot Lemon Pepper Vinegar

There are a lot of recipes out there that use lemon juice in them. We like to use lemon juice also, but why not put a lemon vinegar in the lemon juice's place, instead? Remember, vinegar enhances the flavors of everything else in the recipe. It keeps vegetables crisp, fruit white (not brown), and sauces uniquely different. People won't know what you've added that is different, but they will recognize that it is different and that they like it! This recipe has a hot lemon flavor. Mexican dishes, fish, or vinaigrettes will taste extra special with this vinegar added. We promise.

12 slices fresh lemon (thin)
15 small red Thai Chilies
2 tsp. whole white peppercorns
16oz. (455g) white wine vinegar

Slightly dehydrate the lemon slices following the dehydrating instructions on page 16. You'll recognize by now that the only reason we dehydrate the citrus is to make it flexible enough to roll into the bottle. If you are making a mega bottle of vinegar that has a large mouth on it, don't bother to dehydrate. Roll the citrus into the bottle, mixing them up with the small chilies. Add the peppercorns. Pour the vinegar over the ingredients. Cork tightly. Makes 1 bottle.

Hot Pepper Vinegar

You will find this a useful vinegar to have on hand. In fact, we strongly suggest that this is a must have in your collection. Not only will you have an instant source of hotness for certain Mexican and Oriental dishes, but you will always be in possession of pickled peppers! Just pull one out of your jar and cut off a little to use in your recipe, putting the rest back into the bottle. Look for our hot artichoke dip, garden salsa and many other tantalizing treats that will allow you to enjoy your Hot Pepper Vinegar.

16oz. (455g) white wine vinegar
2 red chili peppers (halved)
2 green jalapeno chili peppers (halved)
1 orange habanero pepper (halved)
1 yellow chili pepper (halved)
2 green Serrano chili peppers
3 springs fresh cilantro
2 green olives
2 tsp. whole peppercorns (mixed colored peppercorns look nice)
3 cloves of fresh garlic (peeled)

Cut peppers and alternately add to bottle to create a nice mixture. Add peppercorns, cilantro, olives and garlic. Pour in vinegar to fill bottle. Cork tightly. Let sit for approximately 10 days to infuse. Makes 1 bottle.

CAUTION: When cutting the peppers, it is very important to wear latex gloves (or something similar to protect your hands). The oil from the peppers gets onto your skin and is difficult to wash off—rather, it has to wear off. We have had many painful experiences with the hot peppers (i.e., taking out contact lenses and licking your fingers). So, vinegar makers, beware!

Lemon Dill Vinegar

We're sure that this will be one of your staple vinegars. The list of ideas for Lemon Dill Vinegar is endless. Talk about a great vinegar for fish! And try our Lemon Dill Vinaigrette. You'll find it's great for salads and as a chicken marinade.

16oz. (455g) white wine vinegar
4-5 springs fresh dill weed (gently rinsed)
5 lemon slices (partially dehydrated—see instructions on page 16)
2-3 cloves fresh garlic (peeled)

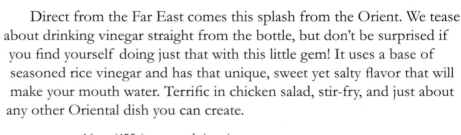

Once lemon slices are prepared, place in bottle interspersed with dill weed and garlic cloves. Pour vinegar over the ingredients and cork tightly. Allow vinegar to sit for approximately 10 days before using. Makes 1 bottle.

Oriental Spice Vinegar

Direct from the Far East comes this splash from the Orient. We tease about drinking vinegar straight from the bottle, but don't be surprised if you find yourself doing just that with this little gem! It uses a base of seasoned rice vinegar and has that unique, sweet yet salty flavor that will make your mouth water. Terrific in chicken salad, stir-fry, and just about any other Oriental dish you can create.

16oz. (455g) seasoned rice vinegar
1-2 stems of lemon grass
2-3 slices of fresh ginger

Prepare lemon grass and ginger and place in a clean bottle. Pour seasoned rice vinegar into bottle and cork tightly. Let sit for approximately 10 days to infuse. Use generously. Makes 1 bottle.

Provencal Vinegar

Many people have asked us what our favorite vinegar is. That's a tough question for the Vinegar Ladies. That's like asking a mother which of her children is her very favorite. You'd feel disloyal if you really answered. But, if we were really pinned down and tickled, this vinegar would probably pop out. It's really quite beautiful to look at. We all feel so talented when we've put together this one. Its fragrance is so appetizing you might want to dab a little behind each ear. And the taste is truly divine. We use it in a lot of our recipes. You'll also find many ways to use this one. So, make it and add it to your staple collection…or you'll be sorry!

2 sprigs fresh thyme
2 sprigs fresh rosemary
3 sprigs fresh oregano
1 sprig fresh basil
1 or 2 fresh bay leaves
2 fresh garlic cloves (peeled)
1 orange peel strip (approximately 1x4 inches or 3x10cm)
16oz. (455g) red wine vinegar
2 teaspoons whole peppercorns (mixed colored)

Place all the herbs into a clean bottle. Carefully add the peppercorns, garlic and orange peel. Add the vinegar. Cork tightly. Store the vinegar 10 days before using. Makes 1 bottle.

Note: A splash of this flavorful vinegar compliments red meat, Italian sauces, and vinaigrettes.

Southwest Chili Pepper Vinegar

This vinegar brings to mind visions of prairie dogs, cactus, and the desert southwest. It is a beautiful combination of fresh herbs and dried Arbol chili peppers. It's a great vinegar to add a little kick to any southwestern dish. Especially good in stir-fry and Tex-Mex style dishes. We especially like it in our Broccoli Bonanza Salad.

16oz. (455g) white wine vinegar
1 large piece of fresh basil
4 sprigs fresh oregano
2 tsp. whole mixed peppercorns
2 cloves fresh garlic (peeled)
8 dried Arbol chili peppers

Rinse herbs gently. Pat dry. Place peppercorns and garlic pieces in the bottom of your clean bottle. Arrange herbs and peppers in bottle. Pour vinegar over your ingredients. Cork tightly. The flavors will infuse into the vinegar in about 10 days. Makes 1 bottle.

Sweet 'n' Sassy Vinegar

We're amazed at how long this vinegar stays looking beautiful. We pulled a bottle out just the other day that was at least 4 years old and it still looked surprisingly good. The flavors truly are sweet (meaning the seasoned rice vinegar) and sassy (meaning the hot Holland chilies). You'll really like the combination. When you use this vinegar in salads such as our Mardi Gras Salad, you'll come to love the taste. And you will notice that this is probably the easiest vinegar of all to make.

7 Holland chilies (long, thin, red)
16oz. (455g) seasoned rice vinegar

Gently wash your chilies. Sometimes this type of chili is hard to find. Ask your grocer to get them in for you. The chilies are slender enough that they will go into your bottle with slicing. Many times the store will have some tiny, red chilies. Those will work too. You'll also notice that we're using seasoned rice vinegar. We like this one because it is seasoned with a small amount of salt and sugar. So, pour the vinegar over the chilies in your bottle. Cork tightly. Allow 10 days before using for good flavor. Makes 1 bottle.

Tangy Citrus Vinegar

The beauty of this vinegar is not only in the way it looks, but in the way it tastes as well. The colors of the four different citrus fruits gently rolled into the bottle makes this one of the most requested vinegars at our classes. Use it straight from the bottle to baste on grilled poultry or use it as a substitute for lemon juice in your favorite recipe. Desserts will benefit from this vinegar, too. Try our Tangy Citrus Vinaigrette and try pouring it over a fresh fruit salad. The vinaigrette will keep your apples and bananas from discoloring.

2 pink grapefruit slices (thin)
4 lemon slices (thin)
4 lime slices (thin)
3 orange slices (thin)
16oz. (455g) white wine vinegar

Follow the instructions on page 16 to slightly dehydrate the slices of citrus. They need to be dehydrated so that they can be pliable enough to roll into the bottle without breaking apart. After you have prepared the citrus, start gently rolling the fruit (like a crêpe) into the bottle. Be sure not to push too hard and break up the meat of the citrus. Also, make sure you vary the colors of your citrus as you insert them into the bottle. Once they are in, it is very hard to change their positions. Pour vinegar over the fruit. Cork tightly. Allow 10 days for the full infusion of flavor. Makes 1 bottle.

Tomato Basil Vinegar

Don't you think that tomatoes and basil are just meant to go together? We knew you'd feel that way, too. Tami grew up in a German household where everything she ate had vinegar in it. Her favorite side dish was sliced tomatoes garnished with fresh basil and covered with apple cider vinegar and a little bit of sugar. So no wonder we came up with this vinegar. It has really become one of our favorites, and it is so easy to make. We're sure you'll keep this on hand at all times—German or not! Also, try our recipe for Tomato Basil Chicken. You'll love it.

7-8 tiny pear tomatoes (yellow and red, halved)
2-3 sprigs fresh basil
3 cloves fresh garlic (peeled)
2 teaspoons whole peppercorns (multi-colored)
16oz. (455g) red wine vinegar

Be sure and gently rinse the tomatoes and herbs. Place them in a bottle. Add the garlic and peppercorns. Pour in the vinegar. Cork tightly. Will be ready to use in about 10 days. Makes 1 bottle.

Starters

Appetizers are so delicious. So why do we save them for special guests and parties? Aren't our families worthy of these delectable treats too? After browsing through the recipes that follow in this section, might we suggest that you plan an "Appetizer Evening" for the ones you love? It only takes a few really good appetizers to create an awesome meal. It would be a fun way to get to know us and our vinegars just a little better. It may also be a way to get your creative juices flowing, you know, start thinking about how you can incorporate some of your newly-made vinegars into your favorite recipes. That's what it's all about, after all, taking regular recipes and turning them into gourmet delights. When you really want to impress, it is important to start your meal off with the perfect appetizer. You'll notice that most of our recipes aren't complicated. Who has the extra time to spend slaving away in the kitchen? We have really tried to create great recipes that require a minimal amount of effort, and yet will have everyone begging for you to share the recipe…and that is the ULTIMATE compliment.

Avocados with a Warm Dressing

This is an amazingly appealing combination. The avocados are served cold, and the dressing that tops them is warm. But more than that, it's the blandness of the avocado meat with the gently spiced dressing that really makes this an unusual and tasty appetizer for any dinner or gathering. This recipe also makes a nice, quick light lunch. Just for you!

4 Tbs. butter
¼ cup ketchup
¼ cup
1 Tbs. honey
2 Tbs. Worcestershire sauce
¼ cup **Hot Pepper Vinegar** (see page 23)
2 avocados

Mix all the ingredients together, except the avocados, in a small saucepan. Bring just to a boil over medium heat, stirring constantly. Cut the avocados in two, lengthwise, and remove the pits and peel. Fill the cavities with the warm dressing. This recipe makes more than most avocado peels can hold, but not more than most avocado lovers can eat! Put the remaining dressing in a small pitcher or bowl and pass with the avocados to be added at will. Serves 4.

Barbecued Pecans

If you are a nut lover, then you'll want to try these unusual pecans. Pack a little baggie in your husband's pocket when he leaves in the morning. Makes a nice little protein pick-me-up and works as a great TV snack.

2 Tbs. butter or margarine
¼ cup Worcestershire sauce
1 Tbs. ketchup
2-4 dashes Tabasco sauce
1½ Tbs. **Sweet & Sassy Vinegar** (see page 26)
4 cups pecan halves
salt to taste

In a small saucepan, melt butter. Add Worcestershire sauce, ketchup, Tabasco sauce and vinegar. Stir until mixed well. Gently stir in pecans making sure you are covering them thoroughly with the sauce. Spread pecans on baking sheet and toast in oven at 400°F (200°C) for approximately 20 minutes, stirring often. Turn out on waxed paper and sprinkle lightly with salt. Makes a great party appetizer that won't fill you up.

Cheeseburger Potato Skins

This is a must-serve recipe when the gang gets together to watch the big football game. A real man-pleaser (we wouldn't recommend it for a ladies social luncheon). But don't try to serve them without the dip. They go together like the Beatles…alone they are alright, but together they are history makers. Great addition to an appetizer buffet when you really want to fill 'em up.

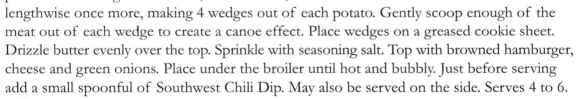

4 large potatoes (baked)
3 Tbs. butter (melted)
1lb. (455g) lean ground beef (browned in vinegar, drained)
¼ cup **Hot Pepper Vinegar** (see page 23)
1 recipe **Southwest Chili Dip** (see page 42)
3 green onions (chopped)
1lb. (455g) cheddar cheese (grated)
Lawry's seasoning salt

Bake potatoes until fork can be inserted easily. Cool. While still slightly warm, slice each potato in half lengthwise. Then, cut each half, lengthwise once more, making 4 wedges out of each potato. Gently scoop enough of the meat out of each wedge to create a canoe effect. Place wedges on a greased cookie sheet. Drizzle butter evenly over the top. Sprinkle with seasoning salt. Top with browned hamburger, cheese and green onions. Place under the broiler until hot and bubbly. Just before serving add a small spoonful of Southwest Chili Dip. May also be served on the side. Serves 4 to 6.

Cinnamon Ambrosia

This is a lovely dish for cool autumn days. Don't know if the kiddies will go for this one, but it is delicious and may be a hit if Grandma is coming for a visit. The beautiful colors shout hayrides and carved pumpkins. A great treat if you're looking to try something new.

⅓ cup lemon juice
¼ cup **Tangy Citrus Vinegar** (see page 27)
¾ cup brown sugar
2 Tbs. corn syrup
⅓ cup honey
¼ tsp. cinnamon
cornstarch to thicken
oranges, bananas, dried cranberries, apples, dates or other fruit of your choice

Combine lemon juice, vinegar, brown sugar, corn syrup, honey and cinnamon in a medium-size saucepan. Bring mixture to a boil over medium heat, stirring constantly. Thicken with a little cornstarch. Let cool. While cooling, peel oranges with a knife, being careful to cut as much of the white membrane off orange meat as possible and slice. Slice bananas and cut apples into thin wedges. Arrange all fruit in a shallow dish. Pour cooled mixture over fruit, cover and let marinate in the refrigerator for 1 hour before serving. Serves 6 to 8.

Crab Nachos

The only way to improve on the flavor of nachos, of course, is to add crab and a little vinegar! These are absolutely scrumptious. In fact, you will want to lick the plate, which is absolutely allowed, as long as no one is watching you do it.

1lb. (455g) imitation crab flakes

1lb. (455g) mozzarella cheese (shredded)

8oz. (225g) cheddar cheese (shredded)

2 large tomatoes (diced)

3 Tbs. **Sweet & Sassy Vinegar** (see page 26)

1 cup finely chopped celery

2 green onions (chopped)

1 tsp. salt

enough sour cream to stick everything together

1 large bag tortilla chips

Spread tortillas on a microwaveable plate. In a bowl, mix all other ingredients together. Sprinkle crab mixture evenly over chips. Melt in microwave or under broiler. Serve hot!

Note: Hot Pepper Vinegar may be substituted if necessary.

Cranberry Salsa

Do you go to as many parties during the holiday season as we do? I mean family and friend get-togethers are fun, but they never seem to end. And, of course, to every one of them you must bring an appetizer or dessert. Well, this season wow all of your party invitations with this new twist on salsa. Some of the ingredients are surprising, like fresh cranberries with tomatoes. But they really taste great together. This salsa is also beautiful with its festive colors. And it's on the sweeter side, so a good salty tortilla chip really compliments the flavor. Make a double batch and save some for yourself. Don't be surprised when it is requested year after year. It has happened to us.

2 cans ready-cut and peeled tomatoes
1 can cranberry sauce
2 stalks celery (chopped)
7 baby carrots (peeled, chopped)
1 large anaheim pepper (chopped)
1 cup fresh cranberries (chopped)
1 medium red onion (chopped)
2 green onions (chopped finely)
½ tsp. dried cilantro
3 Tbs. brown sugar
2 tsp. salt
¼ cup **Hot Pepper Vinegar** (see page 23)
Parmesan cheese

Place tomatoes in a blender and quickly pulse them 2 times (no longer). We just want them to be slightly blended. In a large bowl, mix tomatoes and all other ingredients together. Chill. The cranberries will be hard to chop by hand, so you'll need to use some kind of chopper. Serve with tortilla chips or on top of a baked chicken breast, sprinkled with Parmesan cheese. Makes 4 cups.

Cranberry Zip Dip

Looking for a new dip to use with fruit? Well, if you like cranberries, then we think this will probably tickle your taste buds. Made in the blender, it is quick, easy and simply delicious. But beware of the little punch it packs—that's why it's called Zip Dip! It is particularly good with kiwi slices, apple slices, citrus fruit, and grapes.

14oz. (400g) can cranberry sauce
½ cup **Cranberry Cinnamon Vinegar** (see page 19)
½ tsp. dry mustard
¾ cup sugar
⅓ cup vegetable oil

Mix all of the above ingredients in a blender until smooth. Cover and refrigerate. Enjoy!

Crispy Bacon Squares

Why does bacon have to taste so good? Why does the smell of bacon frying in the kitchen bring everyone running? And why does everyone always want a piece? We don't know! And we're not afraid to say so. But, what we do know is that this little recipe will have the same effect on your guests. They'll sniff it out and snarf it up. So make plenty.

1lb. (455g) bacon (cooked, crumbled)
1 bunch green onions (chopped)
8oz. (255g) grated sharp cheddar cheese
mayonnaise
3 Tbs. **Provencal Vinegar** (see page 25)
very small, square deli bread (rye is wonderful)

Mix bacon, onions, cheese and vinegar in a small bowl. Add enough mayonnaise to make a nice consistency. The deli bread comes already sliced, but if you are slicing your own, make sure to slice it very thin. Arrange bread on a lightly greased baking sheet. Spoon the bacon mixture onto the center of each piece of bread. Place under a low broiler for 5 minutes. Watch carefully because you only want to melt the cheese and brown the top slightly. You'll have plenty with this recipe.

Deep Fried Mushrooms

As good as these mushrooms are, they may not be for you if you are trying to avoid fried foods because you won't be able to stop with just one. They'll call to you from across the room to eat another and another. They're what we call more-ish. It's just impossible to resist. Beware!

½ cup flour
½ tsp. salt
¼ tsp. pepper
3 eggs (beaten)
1½ tsp. vegetable oil
2 Tbs. **Provencal Vinegar** (see page 25)
1½ tsp. water
32 large, fresh mushrooms
1 cup Italian seasoned bread crumbs
oil for deep frying

In a small bowl, combine flour, salt and pepper. Set aside. In another bowl, mix together eggs, oil, water and vinegar. Clean mushrooms with a damp paper towel. Roll mushrooms in flour mixture, dip in egg mixture and then roll in bread crumbs. Place on tray and chill for 1½ hours. Preheat oil in deep fryer to 375°F (190°C). Remove mushrooms from refrigerator and deep fry until golden brown. Drain on paper towel to absorb excess grease. Great served with dipping sauce of Southwest Chili Dip or Ranch Dressing.

Devilish Eggs

Our kids request these at every holiday and sometimes they even invent holidays just so they can have these tasty little devils. There is no limit on how many eggs you are allowed to consume before it becomes impolite, so eat hearty and make any day a holiday.

6 hard-boiled eggs
½ cup mayonnaise
2 tsp. **Hot Pepper Vinegar** (see page 23)
2 tsp. prepared mustard
⅛ tsp. Worcestershire sauce
salt & pepper to taste
paprika

Boil eggs and cool. Shell eggs and cut in half lengthwise. Scoop out yokes and place in a separate small bowl. Add all other ingredients to bowl and mix until well blended. Place hollow whites on a serving platter and gently spoon in yolk mixture. Sprinkle tops lightly with paprika. Chill in refrigerator until ready to serve. Makes 12. (And that's not nearly enough! You'll probably need to double or triple this one.)

Dilly Crab Rounds

Sometimes when you are giving a fancy dinner party it's hard to devote enough time and talent to preparing appetizers that will impress your guests. This one can help—and you don't have to admit how easy they were to create. We want to keep up appearances, don't we?

½ lb. (255g) crab (flaked)
1 cup shredded Swiss cheese
½ cup mayonnaise
1 Tbs. **Lemon Dill Vinegar** (see page 24)
2 green onions (finely chopped)
¼ tsp. curry
1 tsp. lemon juice
⅓ cup canned water chestnuts (drained, chopped finely)
1 can refrigerated biscuits (Hungry Jack)
fresh parsley (chopped finely)

Combine the crab, cheese, mayonnaise, vinegar, green onions, curry, and lemon juice in a bowl. Set aside. Separate the biscuits into 32 rounds. Place the biscuits on a greased cookie sheet. Put a spoonful of crab mixture on each biscuit round. Sprinkle water chestnuts and parsley on top. Bake at 400°F (200°C) for 10 to 12 minutes. Serves 8.

Garden Salsa

You really know that you've reached stardom when one of your recipes is requested at every party, gathering, holiday, super bowl game, and especially when your teenagers and their friends beg for it. So get ready because this is it…our "claim to fame" recipe. The key ingredient, our Hot Pepper Vinegar, allows you to vary the degree of heat from mild to very hot simply by adding more vinegar. You'll never want to buy bottled salsa again. So get ready to be famous because once you serve this to your friends, you'll never have peace again. Seriously.

2 30oz. (850g) cans ready-cut tomatoes
1 small yellow onion (chopped)
2 medium anaheim pepper (chopped, but not seeded)
½ tsp. dried cilantro
½ tsp. dried cumin
¼ tsp. garlic powder
4 green onions (chopped)
1 Tbs. salt
2 Tbs. brown sugar
⅓ cup **Hot Pepper Vinegar** (see page 23)

To begin, place the 2 cans of tomatoes in a blender. Using the pulse button, pulse 2 times and no more. You want the tomatoes to be slightly blended, but still want it to be chunky. Pour the tomatoes into a large bowl. Add cilantro, cumin, garlic powder, salt, brown sugar, and Hot Pepper Vinegar. Mix well. Add chopped green and yellow onions, and anaheim pepper. Mix well. Chill. Serve with your favorite tortilla chips.

Note: The ⅓ cup of Hot Pepper Vinegar will create a fairly mild salsa. If you prefer salsa with a little more kick, simply add more vinegar.

Garden Gazpacho

Aren't you always just a little bit surprised when you take a spoonful of soup and it's not hot? It's a little shocking, but once you get past the temperature thing, the flavors from this gazpacho will make you forget all about traditional soups. It is so refreshing! This would be a great recipe to try at your next fiesta. Olé!

8 Roma tomatoes (chopped)
2 medium cucumbers (peeled, seeded, cut in 2-inch lengths)
4 stalks celery (sliced in 1-inch pieces)
1 medium-sized bell pepper (yellow or orange) (seeded, chunked)
3 Tbs. tomato paste
4 tsp. salt
½ tsp. cayenne pepper
¼ cup olive oil
¼ cup **Hot Pepper Vinegar** (see page 23)
¼ cup **Sweet & Sassy Vinegar** (see page 26)
⅛ tsp. garlic powder
⅛ tsp. onion powder
4 cups tomato juice
freshly ground pepper to taste
½lb. (255g) (cooked small shrimp (peeled) (optional)
1 avocado (diced for garnish)

In a large bowl, combine all ingredients except half of one cucumber, tomato juice, shrimp and avocado. Using a food processor, pulse the vegetables until they are minced, still retaining some texture. Return to bowl and add tomato juice. Chill. Serve in individual bowls garnishing with avocado, shrimp and cucumber (thinly sliced). Serves 4.

Helma's Hot Tamata Juice

The first time we tried this juice we were just starting to create recipes. When served a glass of this delightful concoction, we both readily gulped it down. We were only slightly embarrassed when we were found requesting second and third helpings. Our friend, Helma, felt she had to give us the recipe since we were such great fans. We only improved on it a little bit by adding Garden Blend Vinegar. We're sure you'll love this drink as much as we do.

1 quart (1L) tomato juice
12oz. (340g) bottle cocktail sauce
2 cans small, broken shrimp (drained, rinsed)
2 cups celery (diced finely)
½ cup green pepper (chopped finely)
2 green onions (chopped finely)
¼ cup sugar
3 Tbs. **Garden Blend Vinegar** (see page 21)
1 Tbs. lemon juice
1 tsp. horseradish
½ tsp. garlic salt
½ tsp. salt

Combine all the ingredients in a mixing bowl. Cover and chill for at least 1 hour before serving. Transfer over to a nice pitcher to serve. Plenty for 8.

Grilled Shrimp Wrapped in Bacon

Talk about a simple recipe. The only thing that will tax your brain is remembering to marinate the shrimp the night before. We think bacon and shrimp are a great combo especially when you can cook them outside—less mess, no smells. Your guests and family will love these. They are so easy to just pop into your mouth, you won't realize how many you're eating until it's too late and you're no longer hungry for dinner. So regulate the intake!

20 jumbo shrimp (cleaned, shelled, raw)
7 pieces of bacon
¾ cup olive oil
¼ cup **Lemon Dill Vinegar** (see page 24)
2 Tbs. fresh dill (snipped finely)
paprika
pepper

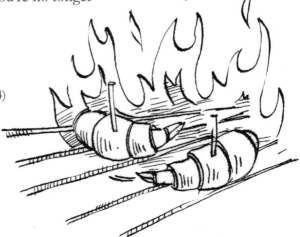

First marinate the shrimp overnight in the following marinade: In a small bowl combine olive oil, Lemon Dill Vinegar, and dill. Place shrimp in the mixture, making sure they are coated well with the marinade, and cover. Refrigerate overnight. If you can remember, stir the shrimp mixture a couple of times while it is marinating.

When you are ready to barbecue, drain the shrimp and lightly sprinkle them with pepper and paprika. Take your 7 pieces of bacon and cut each one into 3 pieces. Take one piece of bacon and wrap it around the shrimp. Use a toothpick to secure. Place on grill on medium heat and cook thoroughly. The bacon should be crisp. Serves 5 to 6.

Hot Artichoke Dip

Simple and delicious. If you're looking for an "alternative-to-salsa" appetizer, this is it. It only takes minutes to prepare, but it tastes like you've spent an hour making it. We guarantee you'll get plenty of compliments on this dish. And if you're looking for a little extra pizzazz, add ¼ pound of fresh crab flakes. Serve with buttery crackers. But it doesn't have to act as just a dip—we have a friend who loves this recipe so much he opts to eat it casserole style. He just takes a huge spoonful of it onto his plate and grabs a fork and goes after it. Anyway you serve it, your family and friends will love it!

2 14oz. (400g) cans artichoke hearts (drained, quartered)
1 cup fresh parmesan cheese (grated)
1 cup fresh mozzarella cheese (grated)
2 cups mayonnaise
1 teaspoon garlic powder
½ teaspoon salt
¼ cup **Hot Pepper Vinegar** (see page 23)
¼ lb. (115g) fresh crab flakes (optional)

Combine all the above ingredients in a bowl and mix well. Be sure that you break up the artichokes a little bit so they aren't in really big chunks. Put in a 2-quart casserole dish that has been well greased. Bake for 30 minutes at 350°F (180°C) uncovered. You want the sides to be bubbling and the middle to be slightly browned. Serve with your favorite crackers and even with tortilla chips. Serves 8.

It Ain't Your Mama's Guacamole

If you are a guacamole lover, well honey, grab a spoon and pull up a chair and we'll eat our way to heaven. It is hard to believe that something so good can be this easy, but it is one of our secrets. Great food doesn't have to be hard, you just need the right recipe. It doesn't show up in the genealogy, but we're sure we must have some South American ancestry, because we love Mexican food almost as much as we love diet coke—and our kids will tell you, we LOVE diet coke. So what are you waiting for? Grab your avocados and Hot Pepper Vinegar and make sure you have plenty of tortilla chips on hand,   'cause you're gonna need 'em!

3 large avocados (peeled, chopped)

1 medium yellow onion (chopped)

1 medium tomato (chopped)

2 small cans chopped green chilies

1 Tbs. olive oil

1 Tbs. **Hot Pepper Vinegar** (see page 23)

2 tsp. salt

Mix all ingredients together except half of the avocados until creamy. Add the remaining avocados and chill. Will keep refrigerated for 5 days. Serve with tortilla chips or with whatever grabs ya!

Mango Salsa

Salsa is not just for tortilla chips anymore. We find it very difficult to function if our refrigerators don't have at least one kind of salsa on hand at all times. The sweet taste of mangoes and pineapple mixed with the hot flavors from the vinegar and pepper create a flavor you will never be able to find at your local grocery store. It's wonderful on omelets, on grilled fish and chicken, or why not mix it with some corn for a side all by itself. How about a chicken and mango salsa salad? Yummy!

1 mango (peeled, pitted, chopped finely)
½ red onion (chopped finely)
1 anaheim pepper (chopped finely)
20oz. (570g) can pineapple tidbits (do not drain)
1 Tbs. lime juice (freshly squeezed is best)
3 Tbs. **Hot Pepper Vinegar** (see page 23)
1 tsp. fresh cilantro (minced)
¼ tsp. cumin
¼ tsp. white pepper
1 tsp. salt
14oz. (400g) can ready-cut and peeled tomatoes
2 green onions (chopped finely)
⅓ cup sugar

In a blender, place the peeled tomatoes. Quickly push the pulse button 2 times (NO MORE). We want the tomatoes to be just slightly blended. Then in a large bowl, combine the tomatoes and all the others ingredients and mix well. Chill. Serve with tortilla chips or over a grilled piece of fish. Makes about 4 cups.

Southwest Chili Dip

This dip is a second cousin to Ranch dressing. They like to hang out in many of the same places…veggie trays, chip bowls, potato bars, etc. Unlike ranch dressing however, our Southwest Chili Dip has a smoky flavor that allows it to stand on its own. We are sure that this is a "Dip" you will want hanging around.

1 cup sour cream
1 cup mayonnaise
⅓ cup **Southwest Chili Pepper Vinegar** (see page 25)
1 tsp. Worcestershire sauce
1 Tbs. your favorite barbecue sauce
⅛ tsp. onion powder
1 tsp. salt
dash of pepper

3 Tbs. ketchup
1 Tbs. chili powder
⅛ tsp. garlic powder

In a medium bowl, whisk the above ingredients together until smooth. Chill. Serve with tortilla chips, onion rings, or as a topping to our potato skins (see page 31). Makes about 2½ cups.

Stuffed Won Tons

Do you have the "appetizer blues?" If so, this recipe will be one you'll cherish. Imagine warm, spicy sausage combined with melted cheeses wrapped up in a crisp won ton blanket. Everyone will look forward to their arrival. No more lil' smokies!

1 pkg. won ton wraps
1lb. (455g) ground sausage (mild or spicy)
½ cup **Provencal Vinegar** (see page 25)
1 cup sour cream
8oz. (255g) cream cheese
2 cups fresh mozzarella cheese (grated)
½ cup freshly grated Parmesan
¼ tsp. onion powder
¼ tsp. garlic powder
salt and pepper to taste

Brown sausage with vinegar in a large skillet. Drain grease. Add cheeses and seasonings. Mix well. Place small spoonful of meat mixture in the center of each won ton skin. Pull the four corners up to the center and press together forming a little pouch. Bakes well in mini-muffin pans. May also be baked on a regular cookie sheet. Spray pan lightly with cooking spray. Bake at 350°F (180°C) for 6 to 7 minutes or until tips of won tons are golden brown. Remove from oven and serve hot.

Tex Mex Dip

If your men folk have been out on the range all day, you can bet they'll be comin' to you with an appetite the size of Texas. So, here is a sure fire way to keep 'em happy 'til dinner is on. Be sure to have heaps of chips on hand when servin' this dish. It'll be a BIG hit, even if you're not in Texas.

1 cup sour cream
2 Tbs. **Hot Pepper Vinegar** (see page 23)
½ tsp. salt
¼ tsp. pepper
2 tsp. taco seasoning
¼ tsp. onion powder
¼ tsp. garlic powder
2 cans plain bean dip
3 green onions (chopped)
3 medium tomatoes (diced)
16oz. (455g) can black olives (drained and sliced)
8oz. (255g) sharp Cheddar cheese (shredded)
1 recipe **It Ain't Your Mama's Guacamole** (see page 41)

In a medium size bowl, combine sour cream, vinegar and seasonings. Mix until well blended. Spread bean dip onto a 9x13-inch (23x33cm) glass dish or other similar size platter. Next, spread guacamole evenly over bean dip. Layer with sour cream mixture, green onions, tomatoes and olives. For the final layer, add the shredded Cheddar cheese. Chill in the refrigerator. Serve with tortilla chips. Makes a Texas size platter of dip.

Tropical Fruit Splash

Fruit is always so beautiful. When it is artfully arranged on a pretty platter there is nothing more inviting to your family or guests. We're finding that many people love to eat fruit as an appetizer. It's light and low in fat. This way, we can all save our fat gram allowance for the main course. Your younger guests will appreciate it, too. They always seem so relieved to actually know and recognize what they are eating.

¼ cup **Tangy Citrus Vinegar** (see page 27)
½ cup mango (cubed)
¾ cup fresh orange juice
1 kiwi (peeled)
1 banana (peeled)
1 cup fresh pineapple (cubed)
1 tsp. poppy seeds
2 tsp. coconut flavoring
1 small can mandarin oranges (drained)
¾ cup sugar
all your favorite fresh fruit (washed, cut up)

In a blender, zip together the vinegar and mango. Add kiwi, banana, pineapple, coconut flavoring, mandarin oranges, poppy seeds, and finally the sugar. Chill for at least 1 hour. Arrange all of your favorite fruit on a platter and drizzle this wonderful sauce over the top. You'll have plenty of splash for quite a large platter of fruit.

Topping It Off

If you haven't already guessed, this is our vinaigrette and dressing section. Before you get too excited to make these recipes, you will want to have made some of the flavored vinegars from the "Vinegars" section of this book. If you haven't done that yet, it might be a good idea to look through the recipes and pick out a few that tweak your taste buds. Start there and you will find that you will quickly become addicted—just like we did.

It is important to remember that the recipes that follow in this section are vinaigrettes or dressings and MUST be refrigerated. They will stay good if kept in the refrigerator for about a week. It is best to store them in plastic or glass containers. You should never keep them in metal containers as they will develop a tinny flavor.

This is really where it all started…making salads and vinaigrettes with our newly created flavored vinegars. It really is our love. Our friends and families love to give us the assignment to bring the salad at any type of gathering. And after you try a few of these, you will understand why. We hope you enjoy!

Balsamic Vinaigrette

This is a great basic vinaigrette recipe. Most good restaurants offer a balsamic vinaigrette, however, some are rather bitter. This one is not—in fact, it's down right tasty. Tami even drinks it, but never before noon!

½ cup balsamic vinegar
¼ cup **Provencal Vinegar** (see page 25)
¾ cup olive oil
¼ cup water
½ tsp. dry mustard
1 Tbs. brown sugar
½ tsp. dried basil (chopped)
½ tsp. salt
⅛ tsp. freshly ground pepper

Whisk together all of the above ingredients in a bowl. Chill. You could also use this vinaigrette to marinate chicken breasts or drizzle on leafy greens.

Banana Poppy Seed Dressing

This is a simple and delicious fruit dip or salad dressing that is different from all the others. We have served it at many of our classes and always got great compliments. Bananas and sour cream make this a very creamy dressing. This is one of those recipes you'll have to share with your friends…because they *will* ask.

2 ripe bananas
1 cup sour cream
½ cup sugar
1 tsp. poppy seeds
3 Tbs. **Tangy Citrus Vinegar** (see page 27)
1½ tsp. dry mustard
1 tsp. salt
1 Tbs. lemon juice
yellow food coloring (just a little to give it nice color)

Mix all ingredients in a blender until smooth. Chill at least 30 minutes prior to serving (longer is better). Great on fruit, greens or both. Try it on our Sunrise Salad (see page 74).

Blue Cheese Dressing

If you are a blue cheese connoisseur, we are certain that this one will pass the test. This is an irresistible accompaniment to most any green salad. Easy to make, but remember...it is best if it is refrigerated 24 hours before you need to serve it. So plan ahead.

¼ cup mayonnaise
½ cup sour cream
2 Tbs. **Lemon Pepper Vinegar** (see page 22)
¼ tsp. dry mustard
½ tsp. Worcestershire sauce
½ tsp. salt
¼ tsp. garlic powder
1 tsp. finely grated onion
3-4oz. (85-115g) crumbled blue cheese

Mix above ingredients together by hand with a sturdy whisk. Chill well and enjoy. Makes a little more than 1 cup.

Blueberry Vinaigrette

If you think you like raspberry vinaigrette, wait until you try this. This is a recipe that we created especially for our Pear Salad. The deep purple color is beautiful, but you would never want to mix it into a salad as it would make the lettuce look gray. It is best drizzled over the top of individual servings. A definite to serve if you are having dinner guests you want to impress.

½ cup **Blueberry Vinegar** (see page 17)
½ tsp. dry mustard
½ cup fresh or frozen blueberries
½ cup sugar
1 tsp. poppy seeds
½ cup oil

Mix all ingredients in blender. You may want to hold out a few blueberries to coarsely chop and add last for texture. Cover and refrigerate until ready to serve. Makes approximately 1 cup.

Cranberry Poppy Seed Vinaigrette

A beautifully delicate, light pink dressing that is perfect for baby spinach mixed with your preference of fruits or vegetables. Similar to raspberry vinaigrette, it is sweet yet tart. A nice surprise for holiday entertaining. It will tantalize the dullest of taste buds.

1 cup **Cranberry Cinnamon Vinegar** (see page 19)
½ cup sugar
1 tsp. dry mustard
1 Tbs. poppy seeds
1 cup vegetable oil

Mix all ingredients together in blender. Chill in refrigerator before serving. Especially good on our Cranberry Walnut Salad (see page 64). Makes approximately 2 cups.

Creamy Garden Dressing

If you are tired of the same old "dip"—and we don't mean your husband—you'll enjoy trying this one. It is a creamy veggie flavored dressing that is terrific on fresh vegetables, pretzels or crackers. A nice change from onion and ranch dip.

1 cup sour cream
1 cup mayonnaise
⅓ cup **Garden Blend Vinegar** (see page 21)
2 Tbs. Lawry's Salad Supreme
2 tsp. salt
1 tsp. dried dill weed
¼ tsp. pepper
¼ tsp. garlic powder

Whisk all ingredients together in bowl and chill in refrigerator. Makes approximately 2 cups.

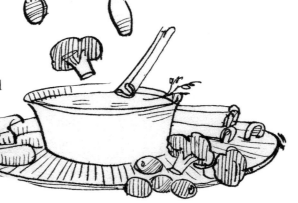

Herbed Pomegranate Dressing

This dressing was created especially for our Holiday Fruit Salad. We remember, way back in the old days, the only time we got a pomegranate was at Christmastime. We loved the tart taste of those messy little seeds and could hardly wait use them in some of our recipes. Pomegranate Vinegar is beautiful with its rich red color and would be a great Christmas gift for your friends. Try this dressing on a leafy salad…add some of those messy little seeds and some pine nuts…you'll love it!

½ cup **Herbed Pomegranate Vinegar** (see page 22)
⅛ tsp. cinnamon
2 Tbs. grape seed oil
½ cup sugar
½ cup plain yogurt
½ tsp. dry mustard

Combine all of the above ingredients in a blender and mix until smooth. Chill. This dressing was especially created to be put over our Holiday Fruit Salad.

Italian Oregano Vinaigrette

This little vinaigrette is very versatile. Obviously, it's wonderful on our Gourmet Chicken Caesar Salad, but there are so many other ways to use it. So you better make a double batch. Try it as a marinade for chicken or drizzle it over vegetables for an extra kick, or lightly brush onto fresh sliced French bread and toast it. We're sure this will become one of your weekly recipes.

1 cup olive oil
3 Tbs. finely grated Parmesan cheese (you know, the kind in the can)
¾ cup **Hot Pepper Vinegar** (see page 23)
1 tsp. sugar
2 tsp. dried oregano (chopped)
1 tsp. salt
¼ tsp. garlic powder
⅛ tsp. freshly ground pepper
1 tsp. lemon juice

Place all ingredients into a blender and mix well. Chill. Serve on everything (a couple drops behind your ears will drive your man wild!). Makes 2 cups.

Mustard Dill Vinaigrette

A great dressing for dill lovers! This unusual vinaigrette combines the spicy taste of Dijon mustard with the unmistakable flavor of dill to create a dressing that you will love to serve again and again. Great on iceberg lettuce and also a fun marinade for fish.

½ cup firmly packed brown sugar
2 Tbs. Dijon mustard
¾ cup **Lemon Dill Vinegar** (see page 24)
1 Tbs. sesame seeds
½ cup vegetable oil
¼ tsp. salt (add more to taste)

In a blender, combine together all ingredients except sesame seeds. Mix well. Stir sesame seeds in with a spoon. Chill well before serving. Makes approximately 1½ cups.

Orange & Rosemary Vinaigrette

Don't expect this to be a mellow vinaigrette. The cayenne pepper and mustard will tip you off to the fact that it is spicy and a little exotic. We created this recipe while on a much-needed vacation in the Caribbean. It goes well with our Mango and Shrimp Salad, but you will love it as a marinade for shellfish or in a pasta salad.

½ cup olive oil

½ cup chicken broth

3 Tbs. **Lemon Pepper Vinegar** (see page 22)

2 tsp. Dijon mustard

1 tsp. fresh lemon juice

¼ cup frozen orange juice concentrate

2 cloves garlic (minced)

¼ tsp. salt

½ tsp. paprika

⅛ tsp. cayenne pepper (add more if you like the heat)

⅛ tsp. freshly ground pepper

1 Tbs. minced fresh rosemary leaves

Whisk the above ingredients together making sure that the orange juice concentrate is completely thawed. Chill in refrigerator. Makes approximately 1 cup.

Oriental Spice Vinaigrette

A very fast, fun and delicious dressing that is great on any type of green salad from the simple to the most elaborate. We have used seasoned rice vinegar (purchased from the local market) and our own Hot Pepper Vinegar together to give it a sweet taste initially, but it warms up with a spicy kick after a few seconds. This is a real winner that will please even the most finicky eater.

1 cup seasoned rice vinegar

½ cup **Hot Pepper Vinegar** (see page 23)

2 cloves garlic (minced)

⅔ cup olive oil

¼ tsp. freshly ground pepper

Whisk all ingredients together in a bowl and chill in refrigerator. This recipe was created especially for our Sweet Pepper Salad (see recipe on page 75). It also serves as a great marinade for mushrooms or chicken breasts.

Provencal Vinaigrette

This is our all-time favorite vinaigrette. It is requested more than any other and is one that you really will want to drink straight from the bottle. It is wonderful on our Bow Tie Pasta Salad (see page 60) and our Caesar Shrimp Salad (see page 61). You could also use it on any green salad and as a marinade for chicken, fish or pork. It is zippy and flavorful. We are sure you will find lots of different ways to use this one.

⅔ cup **Provencal Vinegar** (see page 25)
½ cup water
2 pkgs. dry Caesar salad dressing mix
⅛ tsp. onion powder
¼ tsp. freshly ground pepper
1 tsp. salt
¼ tsp. dried basil (chopped)
¼ tsp. dried thyme (chopped)
15oz. (425g) can peeled tomatoes
1 Tbs. sugar
1 cup vegetable oil
¼ tsp. garlic powder

Combine all ingredients in blender and mix well. Chill in refrigerator. Makes approximately 4 cups.

Note: Sometimes it can be difficult to find Caesar salad dressing mix packets in the grocery store. If you have trouble, you may substitute 2 packages of dry Italian salad dressing mix plus 2 Tbs. of Kraft Parmesan cheese in the green container.

Raspberry Vinaigrette

In recent years, raspberry vinaigrette has become very popular both in restaurants and bottled from the local market. However, it will be a challenge to find one that you will enjoy more than this one. Tart and sweet at the same time, this dressing is great on any type of green salad. A staple for your refrigerator.

1½ cups **Raspberry Vinegar** (see page 17)
1 cup sugar
1 Tbs. poppy seeds

½ tsp. dry mustard
½ cup vegetable oil
½ pint raspberries (frozen or fresh—if you use frozen make sure they are not sugared)

Mix all ingredients together in blender, holding out raspberries. When blended well, add raspberries and pulse the blender 2 or 3 times. Chill in refrigerator. Makes about 2½ cups.

Snappy French Dressing

If you like French dressing, you'll LOVE this recipe. There is no comparison between the bottle dressing you buy at the store and this freshly made dressing (sorry Kraft!).

It's snappy taste enhances salads, especially a chef salad. Tami's husband especially loves this dressing and likes to dip carrots in it!

1 cup vegetable oil
⅔ cup ketchup
½ cup **Berry Vinegar** (we recommend raspberry or cranberry)(see page 17)
½ cup sugar
½ small onion (chopped)
1 Tbs. lemon juice
1 tsp. salt
1 tsp. dry mustard
1 tsp. paprika
¼ tsp. garlic powder
dash of pepper

Combine all ingredients in blender and mix well. Chill in refrigerator. Makes about 3 cups.

Spiced Apple Vinaigrette

The fragrance of this lightly colored vinaigrette will remind you of crunching into a cold, crisp apple on a brisk, autumn day. This vinaigrette has a flavor that is sweet and fruity. It would be especially good on a mixed green salad with diced apples mixed in. Drizzle over apple slices to add flavor and keep them from turning brown. A yummy snack.

⅔ cup **Apple Cinnamon Vinegar** (see page 17)
⅓ cup sugar
1 tsp. poppy seeds
1 tsp. dry mustard
⅔ cup vegetable oil

Mix all ingredients together in blender until thoroughly combined. Chill before serving. Makes approximately 1½ cups.

Note: You may want to add a drop or two of red and/or orange food coloring for eye appeal.

Strawberry Vinaigrette

This recipe is one that you'll need to make copies of because when you serve it you'll be asked again and again to share it. By incorporating the fresh berries in this dressing, it creates a consistency that is great for fruit, salads and even as a fruit dip. This dressing oozes with the aroma of sweet, fresh strawberries. You'll love it, and no kidding, your kids will, too. (Be careful, you may catch them putting it on their waffles!)

½ cup **Strawberry Vinegar** (see page 17)
¾ cup sugar
½ tsp. dry mustard
1 Tbs. fresh minced onion
1 tsp. poppy seeds
⅓ cup vegetable oil
1 pint fresh strawberries (frozen may be used in a pinch)

Combine all ingredients in a blender and mix well. Chill before serving. Makes 1¾ cups.

Tangy Citrus Vinaigrette

Beautifully dressed in bright orange, this vinaigrette vibrates with the flavors of orange, grapefruit, lemon and lime. Wonderful on salad greens or fresh fruit, it is light and refreshing. Remember that vinegar is low in fat, but vinaigrettes are not. Regardless, you will love this recipe for its versatility. Be sure to try it on our Chicken Salad ala Citrus recipe.

½ cup **Tangy Citrus Vinegar** (see page 27)
½ tsp. dry mustard
⅓ cup sugar
1 tsp. poppy seeds
2 Tbs. orange juice concentrate
½ cup vegetable oil
1 tsp. lemon juice
1 drop orange food coloring

Mix all ingredients in blender. Cover and refrigerate. Makes 1 cup.

Salads & Such

With one glance through this section, it should be pretty obvious to you that we had no trouble in coming up with plenty of recipes for this portion of the book. In fact, we had a very difficult time deciding which recipes would make it and which ones would have to wait for later. We have been playing with vinegar for so long now that our husbands sometimes accuse us of having vinegar rather than blood flowing through our veins. However, this is in no way indicative of our sweet, loving nature.

Probably one of the first things people associate with vinegar (once they get past the cleaning issues) is salads and salad dressing. We have taught many classes where ladies (and some gentlemen) had trouble understanding the difference between a flavored vinegar and a vinaigrette. So let's get it straight right now.

A flavored vinegar is straight vinegar that you have flavored by adding herbs, fruit or other spices to give it a unique taste. It contains no oil or mayonnaise. Flavored vinegars do not need to be refrigerated. Vinegar itself is a natural preservative and will stay good indefinitely if stored in a cool place.

A vinaigrette, however, is a dressing made by using the flavored vinegar you have created together with other ingredients which may include oil, mayonnaise, sugar, cheese, etc. These vinaigrettes must be refrigerated and will only last approximately one week.

Now that we have gotten that off our chests, we hope you'll enjoy our salad recipes and the vinaigrettes that complement them.

The Bean Salad

Sometimes you need something simple, fast and tasty. Here is your answer. It has a snappy taste that everyone will enjoy. You can make this recipe the night before, letting it marinate, and be ahead of the game the next day. Even if you only have 30 minutes, with no time to marinate, this salad still tastes great.

2 16oz. (455g) cans green beans
16oz. (455g) can garbanzo beans
16oz. (455g) can white string beans
2 16oz. (455g) cans red kidney beans
1 small red onion (cut in thin rings)
½ red bell pepper (chopped)
¾ cup sugar
⅔ cup oil
⅔ cup **Garden Blend Vinegar** (see page 21)

Drain and rinse the cans of beans. In a large bowl, mix the beans, onion and red pepper together. In a smaller bowl, whisk together the sugar, oil and vinegar. Make sure you whisk the dressing until all the sugar is dissolved. Pour dressing over the bean mixture and toss gently. Cover and refrigerate until it's time to eat. Serves 8.

Bow Tie Pasta Salad

If you are looking for a real crowd pleaser, then this is the salad for you. During the years we were teaching vinegar classes, this was the most requested demo recipe we had. Our families ate this salad practically every week and it is still, to this day, one of their all-time favorites. No need for a special occasion to whip this one up. Make it on Monday and enjoy it for the rest of the week.

16oz. (455g) bag bow tie pasta (cooked, drained)
16oz. (455g) bag frozen peas (thawed)
15oz. (425g) can dark red kidney beans (drained, rinsed)
1 can whole small black olives (drained)
1 cup finely grated cheddar cheese

1 pint (2-cup) basket of cherry or grape tomatoes (halved)
1 cup Hormel bacon bits (these are soft, real bacon pieces)
1 cup **Provencal Vinaigrette** (see page 25)

When cooking the pasta, be sure to refer to the cooking directions on the package. If you overcook the pasta, it will become mushy and fall apart—not very appetizing. After pasta is cool, add remaining ingredients and toss gently, adding vinaigrette last. Refrigerate. Remove from refrigerator approximately 30 minutes prior to serving. Serves 10.

Broccoli Bonanza Salad

This salad is a great substitution when you're tired of green salads. We love to serve it when grilling burgers, steaks and even chicken. It has a sweet taste that complements the seasoned meat well. The Craisins, seeds and cheese give it a fun texture. It is attractive and a crowd pleaser at parties. Don't count on leftovers.

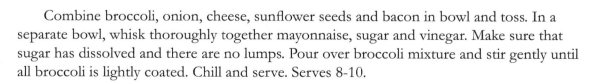

3 cups fresh broccoli florets (cut into small bite-size pieces)
½ red onion (diced)
½ cup Craisins
½ cup salted sunflower seeds (shelled)
½lb. (225g) crisply fried bacon (crumbled)
2 cups shredded mozzarella cheese
1 cup mayonnaise
½ cup sugar
2 Tbs. **Southwest Chili Pepper Vinegar** (see page 25)

Combine broccoli, onion, cheese, sunflower seeds and bacon in bowl and toss. In a separate bowl, whisk thoroughly together mayonnaise, sugar and vinegar. Make sure that sugar has dissolved and there are no lumps. Pour over broccoli mixture and stir gently until all broccoli is lightly coated. Chill and serve. Serves 8-10.

Caesar Shrimp Salad

The simplicity and taste of this salad will completely delight you. If you need a quick and impressive potluck or side dish for your dinner, this is it. Served cradled in a leaf of iceberg lettuce, this salad can be a meal in itself. This recipe calls for fresh, tiny shrimp. However, we have, on occasion, substituted the beautiful, large shrimp when serving it as the main course.

3 large Roma tomatoes (diced)

1lb. fresh shrimp of any size you prefer (cooked and rinsed)

12oz. (340g) bag of shell macaroni

1 small cucumber (peeled and diced)

1 cup **Provencal Vinaigrette** (see page 25)

3 green onions (chopped)

1 cup freshly grated Parmesan cheese

salt and pepper to taste

Cook macaroni according to package directions. (Careful not to overcook!) Drain, and cool in a large bowl. Add shrimp, tomatoes, cucumber, onions and cheese. Make vinaigrette in blender and add to salad ingredients, gently tossing until evenly coated. Chill and keep refrigerated until ready to serve. Serves 6-8 (if using as a side dish).

Chicken Salad a la Citrus

This salad is beautiful served over a bed of leafy lettuce. A nice touch for a ladies luncheon or bridal shower. Light and refreshing with a touch of citrus. This is one of our favorites.

4 skinless, boneless chicken breasts (cooked and cubed)

4 stalks celery (diced)

½ cup slivered almonds

1 small can mandarin oranges (drained)

1 cup red seedless grapes (halved)

4 Tbs. mayonnaise

2 green onions (chopped)

1 package chicken flavored ramen noodles

1 cup **Tangy Citrus Vinaigrette** (see page 56)

salt and pepper to taste

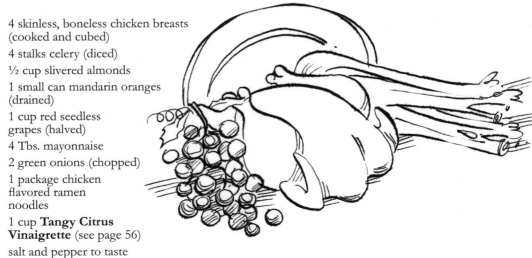

Combine the Tangy Citrus Vinaigrette with the flavor packet from the ramen noodles. Add the mayonnaise. Blend well and refrigerate. In a large bowl, combine chicken, celery, almonds, mandarin oranges, green onions, grapes and the gently broken noodles. Pour chilled dressing over chicken mixture. Toss gently. Season with salt and pepper as desired. Chill until time to serve. Serves 6-8.

Country Potato Salad

This is a great summertime salad that is perfect for a family reunion or a neighborhood barbeque. Traditional in its appearance, the flavor will bring your guests back for a second helping. The subtle blend of vegetables from the vinegar will add the layer of flavor you need to bring out the taste we all strive for in potato salad. This recipe will definitely be a keeper.

10 cups of cooked, cubed potatoes (we like Yukon Gold)

1 bunch green onions (chopped)

6 hard-boiled eggs (chopped)

3 stalks of celery (diced)

Sauce:

2½ cups mayonnaise

3 Tbs. prepared mustard

⅓ cup **Garden Blend Vinegar** (see page 21)

1 Tbs. sugar

½ tsp. celery salt

¼ tsp. onion powder

3 Tbs. milk

salt and pepper to taste

Place potatoes, onions, eggs and celery together in a large bowl. In a second bowl, mix together all ingredients for the sauce. Pour over potato mixture and gently toss until well coated. This salad is best if made 24 hours prior to serving. This allows the flavors to blend. You can also adorn the top of the salad with whole slices of egg and lightly sprinkle with paprika and fresh chopped parsley. Keep refrigerated. Serves 10-12.

Cranberry Walnut Salad

This is the salad for holiday entertaining. Sometimes we need a dish that is easy to put together, yet is extremely impressive. It's quite breathtaking to look at and everyone will want the recipe. The color of the mixed greens in contrast with the red of the dried cranberries and apples are a beautiful combination, especially at Christmastime.

2 10oz. (285g) packages fancy mixed greens
1½ cups dried cranberries
½ cup chopped walnuts (toasted)
2 red delicious apples (chopped into bite size pieces and lightly coated with lemon juice to keep looking fresh)
1-2 cups **Cranberry Poppy Seed Vinaigrette** (see page 50)

Arrange greens on a beautiful tray. Sprinkle nuts, cranberries and apples over the top. Drizzle the Cranberry Poppy Seed Vinaigrette over the top right before serving. Serves 10-12.

Crunchy Chicken Salad

This is the perfect luncheon salad. You can make it the night before and it will taste perfect the next day. We like it served with fresh sliced tomatoes on the side. Or even better, for individual servings you could stuff it in a large tomato and garnish with fresh parsley. Either way, this is a keeper.

4 chicken breasts (cooked, diced and chilled)
1 cup celery (diced)
2 tsp. fresh parsley (finely chopped)
4 hard-boiled eggs (diced)
2 cups red seedless grapes (halved)
½ cup salted almonds (slivered)
⅔ cup **Garden Blend Vinegar** (see page 21)
⅔ cup Miracle Whip
salt and pepper to taste

Combine chicken and celery in a large bowl. Sprinkle vinegar over mixture and let stand for 5 minutes. Fold parsley, salt, pepper, Miracle Whip, grapes, almonds and eggs gently into chicken mixture. Chill well and serve. Serves 6.

Garden Coleslaw

This colorful slaw will awaken your taste buds and surprise your mother-in-law. We use a simple vinaigrette dressing which requires no mayonnaise, allowing the salad to remain fresh and crisp rather than going limp and milky. Extremely easy to assemble. A great salad for outdoor barbeques.

1 large green cabbage (shredded)
1 medium red onion (shredded)
4 carrots (shredded)
¾ cup sugar
¾ cup **Garden Blend Vinegar** (see page 21)
½ cup vegetable oil
1 Tbs. celery salt
¼ tsp. salt
1 tsp. fresh lemon juice

Combine cabbage, red onion and carrots in a large bowl. In a separate bowl, whisk together vinegar, oil, celery salt, sugar and lemon juice. Once sugar is dissolved, pour over cabbage mixture and stir lightly. Chill and serve. Serves 6-8.

Gourmet Chicken Caesar Salad

Every good cook needs an impressive and easy Caesar salad recipe. Well, this is it. You'll find that we've added just about every yummy ingredient we could think of. We think Caesar salads are generally boring, but always loved. So why not give it the kick it needs without too much effort.

1 bag chopped romaine lettuce

1 cup fresh grated Parmesan cheese

14oz. (400g) can artichoke hearts (quartered and drained)

½ cup pine nuts (shelled)

3 Roma tomatoes (sliced)

1 cup croutons

14oz. (400g) can small black olives

¼ cup bacon (cooked crisply and crumbled)

2 chicken breasts (cooked and cubed)

1 recipe **Italian Oregano Vinaigrette** (see page 51)

Combine all above ingredients except the vinaigrette in a large bowl and toss. Gently add the vinaigrette, tossing as you go and making sure the dressing is evenly distributed throughout. You may not need the entire vinaigrette recipe, so add slowly. You can drink the rest!

Holiday Fruit Salad

This is a great wintertime fruit salad. It looks very festive with of all the brightly colored fruit. It would be a great dish to take to a party and is very pretty as an appetizer if served in small, fancy dessert cups. A nice change from the old stand-by green salad, it is lovely served with beef or pork. It has a sweet flavor with a tangy kick. It could even become a holiday tradition.

3 gala apples (diced and lightly coated with lemon juice)

3 green granny smith apples (diced and lightly coated with lemon juice)

4 bananas (sliced and lightly coated with lemon juice)

2 cans mandarin oranges (drained)

1 cup red or green seedless grapes (halved)

1 cup pomegranate seeds
¼ cup raisins (optional but looks nice)
1 recipe **Herbed Pomegranate Vinaigrette** (see page 53)

Lightly toss the above ingredients together in a large bowl being careful not to smoosh the bananas into mush. Drizzle the dressing over the top and gently stir until all fruit has been well coated. Chill and serve. Serves 8-10.

Mango & Shrimp Salad

This is a very showy salad. The colors are beautiful together and would make a great side with a fish entree. Would also be a great main dish for a ladies luncheon. Use this when you really want to impress.

1lb. (455g) large cooked shrimp (shelled and deveined)
2 ripe medium size mangos (peeled and cut into 1-inch cubes)
1 small bag baby spinach
1 small red onion (halved then sliced thinly)
1 small carrot (peeled and grated)
1 recipe **Orange & Rosemary Vinaigrette** (see page 52)

Rinse the shrimp with cold water. Drain well. Combine shrimp, onion and grated carrots in a large bowl and gently stir in half cup of the vinaigrette. Let marinate in the refrigerator for about 1 hour. Just prior to serving, add the mango and the spinach to the marinated shrimp mixture and toss. Add the remaining vinaigrette and serve immediately. Serves 4.

Mardi Gras Salad

This salad is so colorful it looks like a party in a bowl. It has similarities to coleslaw, but is a lot more fun. The dried cranberries and mandarin oranges offer a playful sweetness that puts it in a category all by itself. This recipe makes a large salad…so have a party!

½ head green cabbage (shredded)
½ head red cabbage (shredded)
½ head Chinese cabbage (shredded)
2 cups shredded carrots
1 pkg. ramen noodles (broken up)
1 cup dried cranberries
2 cups salted cashews
2 small cans mandarin oranges

Dressing:
1 cup orange juice
1 cup **Sweet & Sassy Vinegar** (see page 26)
2 cups sugar
1 Tbs. dry mustard
2 Tbs. soy sauce
½ cup vegetable oil
1 Tbs. poppy seeds
¼ cup fresh lemon or lime juice
1 to 2 drops orange food coloring (This is to give the dressing a nice peachy color. Don't overdo it or your dressing will look like Halloween!)

Combine the dressing ingredients in a blender and mix well. Chill. While dressing is chilling, shred cabbage and carrots and combine with the remaining ingredients in a large bowl. Refrigerate. Thirty minutes prior to serving, stir the dressing into the cabbage mixture and return to refrigerator. Serves 12-15.

Oriental Chicken Salad

Everyone loves a good oriental chicken salad—even kids. The slivered almonds and fried wontons add a nice crunchy texture. This is a great side dish or can even be used for a light dinner. It is especially yummy with our Spiced Ginger Dressing. Try it, we know you'll love it.

15 to 20 won ton skins (cut into ½-inch/1cm strips)
1 head of lettuce (shredded)

4 chicken breasts (cooked and cubed)
1 bunch green onions (chopped)
½ cup slivered almonds
2 Tbs. sesame seeds
1 recipe **Oriental Spice Vinaigrette** (see page 53)

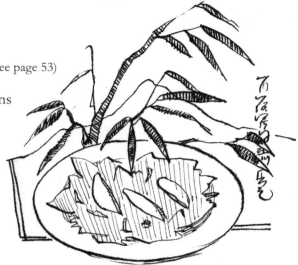

In a large frying pan, fry the won ton skins over medium heat in a small amount of oil just until lightly brown. Remove from pan and drain on paper towel. In a large bowl, combine lettuce, chicken, green onions, almonds and sesame seeds. Add vinaigrette and toss lightly. Refrigerate. Then just before serving, add won ton strips and gently stir into salad. Serves 6.

Party Pasta Salad

Don't you just love it when your kids bring all their friends home and announce that they're hungry. Vinegar Ladies to the rescue! As you can tell, this salad's origin was based on a desperate mom throwing everything in the pantry into one bowl, dressing it and calling it dinner. Surprisingly, it is delicious and will please the hungriest of crowds. They'll think you're amazing…and of course you are!

16oz. (455g) package rotelle pasta (cooked according to package directions and drained)

1 cup freshly grated Parmesan cheese

1 pint grape tomatoes (halved)

1 sweet yellow bell pepper (sliced into thin slices)

1 sweet green bell pepper (sliced into thin slices)

15oz. (425g) can dark red kidney beans (rinsed, drained)

1 small can sliced black olives

1 cup pine nuts (optional)

1 can quartered artichoke hearts (drained)

1 recipe **Italian Oregano Vinaigrette** (see page 51)

Combine all above ingredients in a very large bowl. Toss gently. Add dressing and serve.

Pear Salad with Blueberry Vinaigrette

Having a dinner party and you really want to wow your guests? This salad is the ticket. The flavor combinations are a real palate pleaser, and the blueberry vinaigrette is the crowning touch. Make it often and enjoy.

    1lb. (455g) mixed baby greens
    2 pears (peeled, cored and thinly sliced)
    1 cup sun flower seeds (shelled, roasted and salted)
    1 cup crumbled bleu cheese
    2 cans mandarin oranges (drained)
    ½ red onion (thinly sliced)
    1 cup freshly grated Parmesan cheese
    1 recipe **Blueberry Vinaigrette** (see page 49)

On a large platter or individual serving plates, layer the baby greens, sunflower seeds, blue cheese, oranges and red onion. Carefully arrange pear slices on top. Sprinkle Parmesan cheese over the pears. Lightly drizzle the vinaigrette over the salad and serve immediately. Serves 10-12.

Spinach Salad with Warm Dressing

This recipe was handed down from Tami's mom and is a family jewel. A truly classic spinach salad. As a child, Tami was really grossed out by the warm dressing, but she understands now why all the neighbors raved about her mom's spinach salad. We share it with you and know you'll love it, too.

8 pieces bacon
1 cup brown sugar
1 cup **Tarragon Vinegar** (see Basic Herb Vinegar recipe page 18)
3 Tbs. water
2 eggs (slightly beaten)
1 bag spinach
8oz. (225g) mushrooms (sliced)
8oz. (225g) mozzarella cheese (grated)
1 red onion (thinly sliced)
1 cup cottage cheese (drained)

Fry bacon in large skillet until crispy brown. Remove bacon from skillet and place on paper towel to absorb excess grease. Whisk together vinegar, sugar, water and eggs. Add mixture to the grease in the skillet. Bring to a boil over medium heat. Let boil for approximately 1 minute. Remove from heat. In a large salad bowl, mix together the spinach, mushrooms, onion, cottage cheese and mozzarella cheese. While the dressing is still warm (but not hot), add to salad greens and toss lightly. Serve immediately. Serves 6.

Spinach Salad with Yellow Tomato Vinaigrette

If you enjoy growing your own tomatoes, be sure to add yellow tomatoes to your assortment the next time you plant. Sure, you can buy them in the produce section of most grocery stores, but as we all know, homegrown tomatoes have so much more flavor. This recipe simply glorifies the yellow tomato. It is a basic spinach salad, but it's the dressing that makes it really special. The beautiful color of the yellow tomato combined with the deep green of the fresh basil leaves, looks as wonderful as it tastes. You'll want to serve this one again and again.

> 1 bag baby spinach leaves
> 1lb. (455g) sliced mushrooms
> ½ red onion (thinly sliced)
> ½-1 cup fresh grated Parmesan cheese

Dressing:

> 2 good size yellow tomatoes (diced into small pieces)
> ⅓ cup **Farmers Market Vinegar** (see page 20)
> 3 Tbs. olive oil
> ½ tsp. sugar
> 2-3 fresh basil leaves (finely chopped)
> salt and freshly ground pepper to taste

Combine tomatoes, oil, vinegar, basil and seasonings together in a small bowl. Whisk until blended well. Chill. In a large bowl, toss together spinach, mushrooms, onion and cheese. You can toss the dressing into the salad just prior to serving. However, this dressing is probably best if added to individual servings of salad. Simply place a small bowl of dressing next to the salad and let your guests serve themselves—and believe us, they will.

Strawberry Spinach Salad

This is the perfect salad to make when strawberries are in season. It not only looks beautiful, it tastes terrific, too. It is the perfect blend of leafy greens and the luscious sweetness of the strawberries. The vinaigrette is the crowning jewel and will make your taste buds go snap, crackle, pop! Try this one, you'll wish strawberries were in season year round.

> 1 bag baby spinach leaves
> 1 head romaine lettuce (broken into bite-size pieces)
> ½ red onion (thinly sliced)
> ½ cup fresh grated Parmesan cheese

2 pints (1L) of fresh strawberries (thinly sliced)
1 recipe **Strawberry Vinaigrette** (see recipe page 56)

In a large bowl, gently toss together spinach, romaine, onion, Parmesan cheese and strawberries. In a separate bowl, mix together the Strawberry Vinaigrette. You may want to make the dressing ahead of time and chill it in the refrigerator prior to adding it to the salad. Just before serving, carefully add dressing to salad and toss until evenly coated. You may not need the entire dressing recipe. Too much dressing will make the salad wilt quickly.
Serves 8-10.

Stuffed Artichoke Salad

Tired of serving the same old thing for dinner? Try this fun salad to turn the heads of your family. Not only is this a delicious chicken salad, but the individual artichoke bowls you create are eye catching. The salad can be used as either a nice lunch or a light dinner. Especially great in the summertime when you don't want to heat up your kitchen in the evening. Just make it in the morning, and chill in the refrigerator until you are ready to eat.
Yum Yum!

4 or 5 whole artichokes (you'll want one per person)
4 chicken breasts (cooked and cubed)
1 cup celery (finely chopped)
3 or 4 green onions (chopped)
13oz. (370g) can artichoke hearts (drained, quartered)
1 cup red seedless grapes (halved)
½ cup salted/shelled sunflower seeds
½ cup fresh grated Parmesan cheese
1 cup mayonnaise
½ cup **Tomato Basil Vinegar** (see page 27)
2 tsp. dry Caesar salad dressing mix
2 Tbs. sugar
salt and pepper to taste

To prepare artichokes for steaming, use a sharp knife and cut approximately one inch off the pointed end of the artichoke to create a flat surface. Next, place the artichokes in a steamer with this newly created flat side down. Add necessary water to steamer, along with juice from half a lemon and a pinch of salt. Steam artichokes until you can insert a knife into the stem easily. Remove from heat and cool.

When artichokes are still a little warm, gently open the leaves as if it were a rose that was blooming. Next, remove the soft center leaves, exposing the heart of the artichoke. Using a spoon, gently remove the heart. You should now have what will look like artichoke bowls. Chill these in your refrigerator.

In a large bowl, combine chicken, artichoke hearts (both canned and fresh), celery, onions, grapes, sunflower seeds and Parmesan cheese. Set aside. In a smaller bowl, combine dressing ingredients: Tomato Basil Vinegar, mayonnaise, Caesar dressing mix, sugar, salt and pepper. Mix until well blended. Next, fold the dressing into the chicken mixture. Remove the chilled artichoke bowls from refrigerator and gently fill each bowl with the chicken mixture. Return to refrigerator and chill until ready to serve.

Note: If time doesn't permit putting together the artichoke bowls, you could use this recipe and stuff tomatoes instead.

Sunrise Salad

This salad is a fun combination of fruit and greens. It's also very healthy and great year round. We recommend that we serve it with our Banana Poppy Seed Dressing. It really complements the salad and will ensure that your guests will compliment you. Best to serve individual servings with dressing spooned over the top.

1 head iceberg lettuce (shredded)
3 oranges (peeled and segmented)
2 grapefruit (peeled and segmented) (ruby red gives nice color)
3 kiwi fruit (peeled and sliced)
1 can pineapple tidbits (can use fresh if desired)
1 cup sliced fresh strawberries
½ cup grated coconut
½ cup slivered almonds
1 recipe **Banana Poppy Seed Dressing** (see page 48)

In a large bowl, combine lettuce, oranges, grapefruit, kiwi, pineapple, strawberries and toss gently. Spoon onto individual serving plates. Garnish with coconut, almonds and Banana Poppy Seed Dressing. Serves 8-10.

Sweet Pepper Salad

This quite a showy salad, but it doesn't take any time to prepare. We think it tastes best with our Oriental Spice Vinaigrette. The sweet-hot taste of the dressing over the sweet peppers and cheese gives the salad an unexpected "kick" that will surprise you.

2 bags romaine salad greens

1 sweet red pepper (sliced lengthwise)

1 sweet yellow pepper (sliced lengthwise)

1 sweet green pepper (sliced lengthwise)

1 cup fresh grated parmesan cheese

8oz. (225g) fresh sliced mushrooms

1 can black olives (drained and sliced in half)

1 red onion (sliced thinly in rounds)

1 recipe **Oriental Spice Vinaigrette** (see page 53)

In a large bowl, combine salad greens, pepper slices, mushrooms, olives, onions and cheese. Toss lightly. Add your vinaigrette and toss again. Serve immediately. Serves 8.

Main Attractions

Recently someone asked us how we came up with all these recipes that call for flavored vinegars. Funny thing is…it really was by accident. As we explained in the introduction, our first inclination was to make the vinegars because they were a pretty decoration on our kitchen counter. When it was mentioned to us that you could use them for cooking, we started adding them to all of our favorite recipes. When we did this, we discovered a most delightful secret. Flavored vinegar simply enhances the flavors of all the other ingredients in your recipe and turns "good dishes into gourmet delights!" So if we were asked for any advice, and we LOVE to give advice, we would encourage you to not only try our recipes, but don't be afraid to experiment by adding flavored vinegar to some of your favorite recipes as well!

3-Day Brisket

You really do need 3 days to make this brisket, so plan ahead. But we assure you, it'll be worth the wait. It is amazing that such a tough cut of meat can be so delicious. The vinegar and the liquid smoke will give it a slightly spicy hickory flavor. This would be great served with our baked beans. Special thanks to our dear friend Liz for her willingness to share her family recipe.

3-4lb. (1.5kg) brisket, fat trimmed (size will depend on how many you are fixin' to feed)
3 Tbs. **Southwest Chili Pepper Vinegar** (see page 25)
¼ cup Worcestershire sauce
½ tsp. garlic powder
3 Tbs. liquid smoke

Line large baking dish with foil and place brisket inside. Prepare the marinade and pour over the brisket. You may need to double or triple the marinade to accommodate your brisket size. Cover with foil. Let brisket marinate overnight in refrigerator. Next day, place brisket in oven (still covered) and slow bake for 4 hours at 275°F (135°C) and then 1 hour longer at 350°F (180°C). If you want the brisket to fall apart for sandwiches, slice when hot. If you would rather the meat stay in nice slices to serve with potatoes or another side dish, wait until meat has

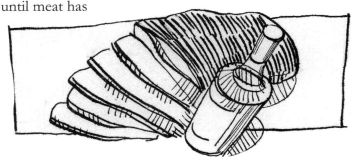

cooled some before attempting to slice. After slicing, return meat to baking dish, cover and refrigerate overnight. Next day, when ready to serve, pour your favorite barbecue sauce over meat and heat for 30 minutes or until hot. Great served on buns or all by itself.

Chicken Penne Pasta

Your kitchen will become your favorite Italian restaurant after you make this recipe. The wine sauce has a heavenly aroma. You'll think you've been transported directly to Italy. Take note that we have used our Provencal Vinegar once again. It goes with just about everything. Well, maybe not ice cream—but everything else!

1lb. (455g) chicken strips
½lb. (225g) small crimini mushrooms (washed and quartered)
⅓ cup flour
1 cube butter
3 Tbs. **Provencal Vinegar** (see page 25)
½ cup sherry (may substitute cooking sherry)
2 cloves garlic (minced)
3 cups chicken broth

1 tsp. dried basil (flakes)
16oz. (455g) bag of penne pasta (cooked and drained)
2 small bottles marinated artichoke hearts (drained)
½ cup freshly grated Parmesan cheese
salt and pepper to taste

In a large skillet, brown chicken and mushrooms in half of the butter. Add garlic, salt and pepper as you brown. When browned, remove chicken and mushrooms from skillet. Add remaining butter to pan and melt. Add flour and stir with fork until you have created a paste. Slowly add the chicken broth while whisking. Bring to a boil. Add vinegar and sherry. Return the chicken and mushrooms to pan along with artichokes and basil. Bring to a boil. Then turn down to simmer and cover for 30 minutes. Spoon chicken mixture over top of pasta. Sprinkle with Parmesan. Serves 6.

Chicken Tortellini Soup

When Tami was on her honeymoon in Mexico many years ago, she was afraid to eat a lot of the food that was served at the hotel. She didn't want to get sick on her newly-wed husband. A version of this soup was served in the dining room. She fell in love with its taste and was very pleased that it set well on her stomach. So, of course, we had to recreate this memorable soup. You'll love it and can feel safe with it.

6 cups water
3 14oz. (400g) cans chicken broth
1 can cream of chicken soup
1 cup carrots (sliced)
1 cup onion (chopped)
3 chicken breasts (cooked and cubed)
2 Tbs. frozen apple juice concentrate
¼ cup **Farmers Market Vinegar** (see page 20)
½ tsp. dried basil (flakes)
½ tsp. dried oregano (flakes)
2 cloves garlic (minced)
9oz. (255g) frozen broccoli florets
7oz. (200g) 3-cheese tortellini (fresh or frozen)

Stir together the water, chicken broth and soup in a large stockpot. Add carrots, onion, chicken, apple juice, vinegar, garlic, basil and oregano. Simmer for 30 minutes. Add the frozen broccoli and tortellini. Simmer for another 5 minutes and serve. Serves 6-8.

Company Chili

Thick and beefy with a hint of bacon and mushrooms, this recipe goes beyond chili. It is worthy of New York City's finest restaurants. You may even want to pull out the china and silver for this one—even if company isn't coming. You'll get rave reviews, we promise.

2lbs. (900g) lean ground beef

1 medium onion (chopped)

12oz. (340g) bacon (uncooked and cut into 1-inch pieces)

¼ cup **Provencal Vinegar** (see page 25)

2 4oz. cans sliced mushrooms (drained)

16oz. (455g) can stewed tomatoes

46oz. (1.3kg) can tomato juice

16oz. (455g) can small red beans

16oz. (455g) can pinto beans

16oz. (455g) can kidney beans

3 Tbs. chili powder

1 Tbs. sugar

2 tsp. salt

1 tsp. paprika

½ tsp. red pepper (optional, depending on how spicy you like your chili)

Brown ground beef, onion, and bacon together in a large pot. Drain grease and add vinegar and all other ingredients. Stir together and let simmer on low heat for 1 or 2 hours or until flavors are well blended. Serves 6-8.

Cottage Chowder

Snow in the forecast? Warm the hearts of the ones you love with this creamy New England style chowder recipe. The bottom of the bowl will bare itself far too soon, so be prepared to serve seconds.

2 6.5oz. (185g) cans minced clams with juice

1 cup onions (finely chopped)

1 cup celery (finely chopped)

2 cups potatoes (peeled and cubed into bite-size pieces)

¾ cup butter

¾ cup flour

1qt. half and half

2 tsp. salt

white pepper to taste
2 Tbs. **Provencal Vinegar** (see page 25)
¼ tsp. dried thyme (flakes)
¼ tsp. dried basil (flakes)
¼ tsp. dried parsley

Place potatoes, onions and celery in medium size pot. Drain clam juice over vegetables and add enough water to barely cover vegetables. Cook on medium until you can insert a fork into potatoes. (You want the potatoes to still be firm, so don't overcook!) In separate bowl, melt butter in microwave. Stir flour into melted butter until well mixed. This will form a roux. Add half and half, salt, vinegar, and spices to vegetable mixture. Add clams and bring to a simmer. Then slowly stir in the roux. Heat thoroughly. Ready to serve. Makes approximately 2 quarts.

Cranberry Pork Chops

It seems like everything you eat during the holiday season is beef or ham. Every party has a buffet with these two meats. Well, liven up your holidays with pork instead! Try this with pork tenderloin pieces for a buffet. They are easier to handle, especially when you can scoop up the pork pieces with plenty of this yummy sauce.

½ cup flour
½ tsp. salt
½ tsp. freshly ground pepper
4 pork chops
1 Tbs. olive oil
2 tsp. minced garlic
1 cup onions (chopped)
1 cup fresh mushrooms (sliced)
1 cup fresh or frozen cranberries (coarsely chopped)
1 can ready-cut tomatoes (drained)
½ cup white cooking sherry
1 cup chicken broth
¼ cup soy sauce
1 tsp. sugar
3 Tbs. **Cranberry Vinegar** (see page 17)

Combine flour, salt and pepper in a shallow dish. Coat chops with flour mixture shaking off excess. Heat oil in a large skillet over medium heat. Add the chops and brown them on both sides—about 5 minutes each side. Transfer to a plate. Add garlic, onions, mushrooms, cranberries and tomatoes to the skillet and sauté for about 2 minutes on low heat. Add sherry, broth, soy sauce, vinegar and sugar. Turn heat up slightly and bring to a boil. When mixture comes to a boil, reduce heat to low, add back the chops. Cover and simmer for 30 minutes. Then turn chops over in sauce and cook for another 30 minutes. Serve immediately.

Creamy Dilled Salmon

You've heard of the salmon run? Well, anyone who knows you are serving this scrumptious dish for dinner, will come running for sure. Therefore, we feel we must issue a warning with this recipe: Be very careful who you tell when serving this dish for you are likely to end up with several unexpected dinner guests.

1 large fillet of salmon
⅓ cup **Lemon Dill Vinegar** (see page 24)
1 lemon (sliced)
1 tsp. dried dill weed
mayonnaise (enough to spread a light coat on top of salmon fillet)
lemon pepper to taste

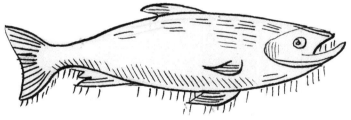

Place your fillet of salmon in a shallow baking dish lined with tinfoil. (Be sure to spray your tinfoil lightly with Pam before placing salmon on it.) Drizzle vinegar over the fillet. Spread a light layer of mayonnaise over the entire fillet. Sprinkle lemon pepper and dill weed over the mayonnaise. Arrange the lemon slices on top. Cover with tinfoil. Bake at 350°F (180°C) for 30 minutes or until salmon is no longer translucent. Serve hot. This recipe is very easy to adapt to large or small dinner parties. For a great summer dinner, try this one on the grill. Just double up the tinfoil—no pan necessary!

Fettuccine Parmesan

Add an international flare to lunch or dinner with this recipe. If you have been just too busy to plan ahead, this is a great last-minute meal. It can be served as the main course with a side veggie and some nice bread or as a side dish to accompany a meaty entrée. Either way, even with kids, this one will be a favorite.

16oz. (455g) package fettuccine pasta
1 cube butter (softened to room temperature)
1 cup heavy cream
1 cup fresh grated Parmesan cheese
¼ tsp. garlic salt
2 Tbs. **Lemon Pepper Vinegar** (see page 22)
lemon pepper and salt to taste

In a large microwave safe bowl, mix butter, cream, garlic salt and vinegar. Cook pasta according to package directions and drain. While pasta is still hot, pour into butter mixture and stir. Add the Parmesan cheese and mix thoroughly. Microwave on high for 1 minute. Stir and serve. Serves 4-6.

Hearty Beef Stew

This is the perfect dinner recipe for busy moms and husbands with big appetites. Throw it together in the morning while the kids are eating Froot Loops, put it in the oven and forget it until dinnertime. Your family will think you are magical. You won't have to call the family to dinner; the aroma will have them circling the kitchen like vultures.

3lbs. (1.4kg) lean stew meat
2 cans cream of mushroom soup
1 can cream of chicken soup
2 cans water
14oz. (400g) can beef broth
1 cup celery (chopped)
1 cup carrots (chopped)
4 medium potatoes (peeled and cubed)
2 dried bay leaves
½ cup **Provencal Vinegar** (see page 25)
8oz. (225g) fresh mushrooms (sliced)
3 Tbs. beef soup base
1 pkg. Lipton Onion Soup Mix
salt and pepper to taste

Mix all ingredients in a large, heavy roasting pan. Stir well. Cover and bake at 275°F (135°C) for 6-8 hours. Baking time may be decreased if cooked at a slightly higher temperature. Serves 6.

Mama's Spaghetti Sauce

This is a hearty tasting marinara sauce that will convince your family that somewhere in your genealogy, you must have Italian ancestors. It is a meat and mushroom sauce that can be served over any variety of pasta, but we prefer it served over angel hair. Quick and easy to prepare and can be made earlier in the day, refrigerated and then reheated when ready to eat. Freezes well.

2lbs. (900g) lean ground beef
¾ large yellow onion (chopped)
6 8oz. (400g) cans tomato sauce
¼ cup **Provencal Vinegar** (see page 25)
1 Tbs. balsamic vinegar
½ tsp. dried oregano (powder)
¼ tsp. dried thyme (powder)
¼ tsp. dried basil (powder)
2 dried bay leaves
1lb. (455g) sliced fresh mushrooms
¼ tsp. garlic powder

Brown the beef and onion in a large skillet. Add salt and pepper to taste. Drain grease and add remaining ingredients. Stir together well and allow to simmer 30 minutes to 1 hour. Serves 6.

Manicotti

Growing up, did you have a neighbor or maybe a friend whose mom was an amazingly good cook? Well, we did and funny thing, that is where this recipe originated. We've enjoyed this dish for many years (we're not going to say exactly how many), and we love it as much today as we did way back when we were kids.

2lbs. (900g) lean ground beef
2 cloves garlic (minced)
1 tsp. salt
¼ tsp. pepper
¼ cup **Provencal Vinegar** (see page 25)
1 box of large pasta shells or tubes
2½ cups cottage cheese
⅔ cup mayonnaise
12oz. (340g) mozzarella cheese
(shredded)
1 cup fresh grated Parmesan cheese
1 Tbs. **Provencal Vinegar**
salt to taste
2 bottles of your favorite spaghetti sauce

Brown the ground beef with the garlic, ¼ cup of vinegar and salt and pepper. Drain grease. Cook pasta according to package directions and drain on sheet of wax paper. Be sure to not overcook the pasta. Set aside. Add to meat: cottage cheese, mayonnaise, mozzarella, 1 Tbs. vinegar and salt to taste. Mix well. Gently stuff cooked pasta shells with ground beef mixture. In a shallow casserole dish, pour a small amount of spaghetti sauce to cover bottom. Arrange stuffed shells in dish and pour enough sauce over top to cover well. Cover with foil and bake at 350°F (180°C) for 15 minutes. Remove foil and sprinkle with Parmesan cheese. Bake for another 15 minutes or until bubbly. Serves 6-8.

Pineapple Barbecue Ribs

This is a great recipe to pull out for the Fourth of July or any other summertime back-yard party. This is a chunky barbecue sauce that could be used on chicken as well. Our husbands love to be in charge of the grill and if given this sauce, they can take all the credit for ribs that make you want to roll up your sleeves and dive right in!

6lbs. (2.7kg) baby back ribs (you can use other varieties is you choose)

Sauce:

1 cup fresh pineapple (diced into very small pieces)

1 can ready-cut tomatoes

2 Roma tomatoes (diced into very small pieces)

1 medium yellow onion (diced)

4 garlic cloves (minced)

2 red chili peppers (seeded and diced)

½ cup soy sauce

½ cup pineapple juice

¼ cup Worcestershire sauce

2 Tbs. dark molasses

2 Tbs. Dijon mustard

¾ cup **Berry Vinegar** (see page 17)

½ cup brown sugar

¼ tsp. freshly ground pepper

½ tsp. salt

Place all ingredients except ribs in a large saucepan. Simmer on medium heat for 30 minutes. Cool. Place ribs in a shallow baking dish and pour sauce over the top. Coat well. Bake at 225°F (110°C) for 3 to 4 hours. Transfer ribs to barbeque grill on low heat for approximately 30 minutes. Use sauce in baking dish to baste ribs. Serve hot with our yummy Country Potato Salad (see page 63).

Polynesian Chicken

When you serve this recipe, your family will be looking around for the hula dancers because they'll think they're at a luau. It really brings a hint of the South Pacific to your dinner table. Can easily be doubled or tripled for a party.

4 to 5 raw chicken breasts (cut into small pieces)

1 large green pepper (chopped into ½ inch pieces)

15oz. (425g) can chicken broth

1 Tbs. soy sauce

½ cup honey

½ cup **Tangy Citrus Vinegar** (see page 27)

juice from half of a lemon

½ tsp. Worcestershire sauce
⅓ cup ketchup
16oz. (455g) can pineapple tidbits (retain juice in separate bowl)
3 Tbs. butter
3 Tbs. cornstarch
paprika, salt and pepper to taste

In a very large skillet, brown chicken pieces in butter, sprinkling with salt, pepper and paprika. Add green peppers. After browned, remove chicken and peppers from pan. Add to skillet chicken broth, honey, lemon juice, ketchup, soy sauce, vinegar, Worcestershire sauce and pineapple juice. Bring to a boil. Put cornstarch in a small glass and add just enough water to make it liquid. Stir into the boiling mixture. Bring back to a boil. Add pineapple pieces, chicken and green peppers. Cover. Cook on simmer for 30 minutes. Serve over a bed of rice. Serves 6.

Pork Chops Dijon

These may just be the best pork chops you've ever eaten! Truly a unique flavor. Maybe not a kid pleaser (depends on how picky they are), but adults will love the creamy Dijon sauce which is served over the chops.

4 ½-inch (1cm) thick pork chops
2 Tbs. butter or margarine
⅓ cup **Shallot Vinegar** (see **Basic Herb Vinegar** page 18)
1½ Tbs. Dijon mustard
2 cups heavy cream
salt and pepper to taste

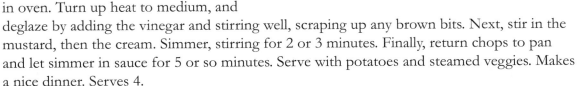

Melt butter in large frying pan over low heat. Add pork chops, seasoned with salt and pepper, and cook, still over low heat, turning occasionally, until done. Remove from pan and keep warm in oven. Turn up heat to medium, and deglaze by adding the vinegar and stirring well, scraping up any brown bits. Next, stir in the mustard, then the cream. Simmer, stirring for 2 or 3 minutes. Finally, return chops to pan and let simmer in sauce for 5 or so minutes. Serve with potatoes and steamed veggies. Makes a nice dinner. Serves 4.

Provencal Pot Roast

Does your Sunday roast need a little lift? Well, look no further. Probably the simplest flavor boost to any roast is a little Provencal Vinegar. And you can take our word for it, your family will definitely notice. The vinegar not only adds wonderful flavor to your meat, it also acts as a natural tenderizer. Don't wait too long before you try this one.

3-4lb. (1.5kg) eye of round roast (or any other nice cut)

¼ cup **Provencal Vinegar** (see page 25)

4 cups au jus

your regular seasonings to taste such as seasoning salt, herbs, freshly ground pepper, etc.

Place your roast in roasting pan and poke with a meat fork several times. Drizzle the vinegar over the roast and then add your favorite seasonings as listed above. We like to slow cook our roasts, which means that we usually brown it slightly in butter before we season and bake it. Pour au jus into the bottom of roasting pan. Then bake it at 300°F (150°C) for about 4 hours. You may add your vegetables, such as potatoes and carrots after 3 hours. The vegetables will absorb all of the wonderful herb flavors from the vinegar. Be sure to use the drippings for your gravy…it will be sensational!

Spring Treasure Pasta

Doesn't it make you feel great when your family would choose to eat at home rather than go out to a restaurant? This dish is just what the recipe says, a real treasure. And also a pleasure if you like asparagus, mushrooms and shrimp. Make any night a special occasion by serving this for dinner.

1 cube butter

2 cloves garlic (crushed)

1lb. (455g) (crimini mushrooms (quartered)

1-2 lbs. (455-900g) fresh asparagus (cut into 1-inch pieces)

1-2 lbs. (455-900g) shrimp (fresh or frozen)

2 cans artichoke hearts (quartered)

1 can chicken broth
1 Tbs. chicken base
3 Tbs. **Tomato Basil Vinegar** (see page 27) or **Provencal Vinegar** (see page 25)
2 cups freshly grated Parmesan cheese
16oz. (455g) package of your favorite pasta
salt and pepper to taste

Cook pasta according to package directions, drain, rinse and set aside. In a very large skillet, melt butter and sauté garlic over medium heat. Add mushrooms and vinegar, cover and sauté for approximately 5 minutes. Next, add asparagus pieces and cover again until asparagus is slightly tender. Next add artichoke hearts, chicken broth, and chicken base. When heated thoroughly, stir in pasta, add shrimp and salt and pepper to taste. Heat through (this will take about 1 to 2 minutes). Remove from heat. (If you leave on heat too long, it will make your shrimp tough). Gently toss in 1 cup of the cheese reserving the final cup to garnish individual servings. Spoon onto individual plates, garnish with cheese and serve hot. Serves 6-8.

Steak & Everything

This recipe has been a family tradition for many years and is requested every summer at the annual camping trip/family reunion. Sure to satisfy the heartiest appetite and can easily be doubled or tripled to accommodate a crowd. A great meal at any time of year.

3lb. (1.5kg) tip roast or other nice cut of beef (slice this very thinly, it is easiest to do with an electric slicer while the roast is still frozen)
1lb. (455g) provolone cheese (thinly sliced)
1 medium onion (finely chopped)
2 small cans sliced mushrooms with juice
6 hoagie type buns
2 Roma tomatoes (diced)
¼ cup **Provencal Vinegar** (see page 25)

Heat large griddle and place sliced roast evenly over surface. While meat is browning, add seasonings (salt and pepper) and vinegar. Once meat is browned, remove from pan and place in a bowl. There is usually someone who doesn't want onions or mushrooms in their sandwich, so this makes it easy to make 1, 2 or 3 sandwiches at a time. Place enough meat back on the griddle for the number of sandwiches you are going to make.

Add the desired ingredients (i.e. mushrooms, onions, or cheese). (A little mushroom juice is good to moisten the meat.) Chop and turn mixture until all ingredients are hot and cheese is melted. Place on buns and top with chopped tomatoes, salt and pepper. (Another nice touch is to spread melted butter on open buns and toast lightly in the oven before adding meat mixture). Serves 6.

Sweetly Sour Meatballs

This is a snappy little main dish or appetizer that is simple to prepare and sure to please.

Would be a great dish to serve during the big football game because it's a real man pleaser…he won't even care if his team isn't winning…well, maybe not. But, his tummy will be happy, even if his soul is sad. Special thanks to our dear friend Kay, who shared this fun recipe from her kitchen.

2lbs. (900g) lean ground beef
2 eggs
1 cup oatmeal
½ small yellow onion (chopped)
1lb. (455g) sliced bacon
1 tsp. salt
¼ tsp. pepper

Sauce:

¾ cup **Blueberry Vinegar** (see page 17)
¼ cup **Hot Pepper Vinegar** (see page 23)
1 tsp. prepared mustard
2 cans tomato soup
3 cups brown sugar

Mix raw ground beef, eggs, oatmeal, onion, salt and pepper in a bowl. Form mixture into golf-ball size meatballs. Cut bacon strips in half and wrap a piece around each meatball, securing it with a toothpick. Place meatballs in a shallow baking dish. Mix ingredients for sauce in a small bowl and whisk together until smooth. Pour over meatballs. Bake for approximately 1 hour at 350°F (180°C). Serves 6-8. Great accompaniment to white rice.

Tomato Basil Chicken

It may sound like a line, but our families really enjoy our recipes. Sure, everyone has their favorite and well, this dish is Kailee's. It has a very mild creamy tomato and basil flavor. She loves it served over a bed of egg noodles. So when mom wants to be the hero of the day… Tomato Basil Chicken is dish.

4 single chicken breasts

3 Tbs. butter

2 cloves garlic (minced)

salt and pepper to season

1 cup orange, red or yellow tomatoes (diced)

⅓ cup **Tomato Basil Vinegar** (see page 27) (can use **Provencal Vinegar** in a pinch, see page 25)

2 cups heavy cream

¼ cup fresh basil leaves (chopped)

1 Tbs. chicken soup base

½ cup fresh sliced mushrooms

Melt butter in large skillet and sauté garlic. Add chicken breasts and season with salt and pepper. Cook on each side for approximately 5 minutes or until golden brown. Add vinegar, tomatoes, cream, basil and mushrooms. Cover and let simmer for 5 to 10 minutes. This recipe can be also be served over pasta. Serves 4.

Turkey Noodle Soup

It seems like every time we have a turkey dinner there are turkey leftovers, which is great for a couple of days. Then everyone is tired of cold turkey sandwiches and you just end up throwing the rest away. Well, no more. Now you can make turkey noodle soup! Although, you may want to throw that left-over turkey in the freezer for a week or two—you know, turkey overload. But when you feel the time is right, this is a great soup to warm up those hungry tummies.

4 cups cooked turkey chunks
12oz. (340g) package frozen peas and carrots
1 can cream of mushroom soup
2 cans cream of chicken soup
½ cup onion (chopped)
1 cup celery (chopped)
3 quarts water
¼ cup **Farmers Market Vinegar** (see page 20) or **Garden Blend Vinegar** (page 21)
5 Tbs. chicken soup base
1lb. (455g) egg noodles

In a large stockpot, bring water, chicken base, vinegar, onion and celery to a boil. Cook until celery is tender. Stir in soups. When well mixed, add noodles and cook until soft. Approximately 15 minutes prior to serving, add turkey, peas and carrots. Serves 6-8. You may substitute chicken for turkey if desired.

Turkey Tacos

This is a great recipe if you are watching your waistline. The low-fat turkey is substituted where ground beef usually lives. Substituting the turkey for beef in other recipes is one way to cut out those extra calories. We have found that the taste is a little bit different, but won't leave you disappointed. You'll love the spicy flair of this recipe and might want to turn it into your favorite taco salad. Enjoy!

1lb. (455g) ground turkey
1 small yellow onion (chopped)
2 tsp. chili powder
1 cup salsa
1 small can green chilies (diced)
¼ cup **Southwest Chili Pepper Vinegar** (see page 25)
1 can whole kernel corn (drained)
½ red bell pepper (diced)
10 flour tortillas
3 cups shredded cheddar cheese
3 cups shredded lettuce

Brown ground turkey in a skillet over medium heat. Cook until turkey is no longer pink. Add onion, chili powder, vinegar, chilies and red pepper. Cook for two minutes. Add salsa and corn. Cook for an additional 5 minutes. Spoon into tortillas and smother with cheese. Mmmmm good! Serves 4-6.

Veggie Soup Olé

As moms, we like to make sure our families are eating healthy. Sometimes the last thing they are interested in eating are vegetables. This recipe, with its Mexican flair, is so delicious, they won't realize that they are getting a mega dose of veggies. A big pot of soup on the stove will bring the busiest of families together, even if it's just for a few minutes.

1lb. (455g) lean ground beef
1 small yellow onion (chopped)
3 carrots (peeled and sliced)
3 celery stalks (chopped)
2 small zucchini (sliced)
1 small yellow squash (sliced)
1 red bell pepper (chopped)
3 new potatoes (cubed into bite-size pieces)
1 cup broccoli florets
1 can corn (drained)
32oz. (900g) can stewed tomatoes
1½ quarts (1.5L) water
4 Tbs. **Hot Pepper Vinegar** (see page 23)
6oz. (170g) can tomato paste
2 tsp. lemon juice
1 Tbs. salt
1 package milt taco seasoning mix
1 Tbs. Worcestershire sauce
2 tsp. beef base
2 tsp. dried parsley
½ tsp. pepper
¼ tsp. onion powder

Brown ground beef and onion. Drain grease. In a large stockpot, combine all the above ingredients, adding the browned ground beef last. Simmer for 2 hours. If you want more broth in your soup, you may add an additional can of tomato juice. Serve hot.

On the Side

 e've decided that side dishes are one of a hungry woman's best friends. If you were at a dinner party and while dishing up your plate, took four helpings of the entrée, the hostess might look at you and think "PIG"! However, if your plate is heaping with ten different side dishes, you would simply be complimenting the cook. We love our side dishes! The more the merrier. They are a great way to make your main dish go a little further. When unexpected company shows up at dinnertime, quickly throw together another side dish and call it good.

In this section, you will find both hot and cold side dishes that of course have an extra special flavor because of the vinegar that has been added to them. If you are working your way through this book, then you should be practically perfectly pickled by now and are probably starting to add vinegar to some of your old favorite recipes as well. Good for you. We knew it would happen; we've seen it a thousand times. Go get 'em!

Annie's Fried Cabbage

This is not a low-fat dish, so dieters beware. But no one ever said Heaven was fat free. Annie's little girls love this dish and that tells you something when kids will eat cabbage. The bacon and Provencal Vinegar give the red cabbage a wonderfully tart flavor. The preparation time is minimal and that's always a good thing. We whole-heartedly recommend this dish. It's especially nice with pork or beef.

1 head red cabbage (cut out heart, quartered, then sliced ½ inch thick)
1 large white onion (chopped)
1lb. (455g) bacon (cut into 1 inch pieces)
2-3 cloves fresh garlic (minced)
½ cup **Provencal Vinegar** (see page 25)
freshly ground black pepper to taste

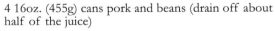

In a large frying pan, fry bacon pieces. When crispy and brown, remove from pan and drain the pieces on a paper towel. Remove half the grease from the pan. Fry onion and garlic in remaining grease. When golden brown, add back the bacon and the sliced cabbage. Add desired pepper to taste. Pour in the vinegar and stir. Reduce heat to simmer, cover and steam for approximately 5 minutes. Remove lid, give the whole thing a good stir and replace lid. Continue cooking until cabbage is slightly wilted but still crisp (approximately 15 minutes). Great served with crusty bread. Serves 6-8.

Baked Beans

You may think that "baked beans are just baked beans," but you haven't tasted OUR baked beans. It's a very traditional recipe with a little surprise—our blueberry vinegar. Yes, we said blueberry. The sweetness of the berry vinegar is the perfect compliment to the barbecue sauce and onions.

4 16oz. (455g) cans pork and beans (drain off about half of the juice)
1 medium yellow onion (chopped)
1lb. (455g) bacon (fried crisp and crumbled) (reserve drippings)
2 Tbs. ketchup
2-3 Tbs. your favorite barbecue sauce
1½ Tbs. prepared mustard (heaping)
½ cup brown sugar

½ tsp. balsamic vinegar
1½ Tbs. **Blueberry Vinegar** (see page 17)
2 Tbs. bacon drippings

Combine all ingredients in a heavy pot and mix well. Can be mixed together a day in advance. Bake covered for 3 to 4 hours at 350°F (180°C). Remove lid for last 30 minutes of cooking time. This will allow the beans to thicken up nicely. Serves 8-10.

Note: If desired, green peppers and pineapple tidbits may be added.

Caesar Tortellini

We are always in a hurry. Aren't you? There just doesn't ever seem to be enough time to keep things clean, run errands, write your vinegar book, let alone sleep...but the real kicker for us is when 4 o'clock rolls around. Dinner and fast have to be synonymous at that time. Try this tortellini dish with a broiled piece of meat. It's easy and will make you feel like you've accomplished something better than macaroni and cheese.

9oz. (255g) pkg. refrigerated cheese-filled tortellini
2 cups small broccoli florets
1 medium tomato (coarsely chopped)
⅓ cup sour cream
¼ cup water
¼ cup **Southwest Chili Pepper Vinegar** (see page 25)
1 pkg. dry Caesar salad dressing mix

Cook tortellini according to package directions. They are quick to cook. Add broccoli to the boiling tortellini the last minute or two. Drain. In a bowl, stir together sour cream, water, vinegar, Caesar mix until smooth. Microwave for 30 seconds to heat. Combine cooked tortellini, broccoli, and tomato in a large bowl. Add sour cream mixture and toss gently. Serve. This side is also very good served cold with a good ol' sandwich. Serves 6.

Creamy Beans with Bacon

Everyone knows and loves the "old stand-by" green bean casserole. We know that Thanksgiving wouldn't be the same without it. But we decided that it was time the good ol' boy stepped down a few notches, and we created the new and exciting version. The zippy vinegar mixed with the sour cream and bacon will bring you out of your side dish rut.

1½lbs. (680g) fresh green beans (snapped into 1-inch pieces)
1½ cups water
½ tsp. salt
1lb. (455g) uncooked bacon (cut into small pieces)
1 medium yellow onion (chopped finely)
2 Tbs. flour
4 Tbs. **Farmers Market Vinegar** (see page 20)
⅔ cup sour cream

In a large pot bring water and salt to a boil. Add the beans and cook until tender, drain. In a large frying pan, fry bacon until crisp. Add onion and sauté until transparent. Add flour. Mix well. Add vinegar and sour cream. Again mix well. Add the drained beans and blend. Cover and let stand for 5 minutes. Serves 6.

Creamy Chive Potatoes

You may want to double or triple this recipe just so you can have leftovers for tomorrow, and the next day, and the next. There is just nothing better than thick, creamy, buttery mashed potatoes with a hint of chives—yum! May not be for you if you're watching your waistline…well, maybe you could have just a little.

5 or 6 large potatoes
(baking size)
¾ cup sour cream
1½ Tbs. **Chive Blossom Vinegar** (see page 19)

heavy cream
butter (melted)
dash garlic powder
salt and pepper (to taste)

In a large stock pot, boil potatoes until tender. Mash potatoes to your liking, using the cream and butter to achieve the right consistency. Add sour cream and seasonings. Stir until well blended. Best served HOT. You may sprinkle with chopped, fresh chives.

Cucumbers in Sour Cream

This is an old traditional German recipe that was shared with us by a dear friend. Using vegetables from our gardens in the summertime gives us a sense of accomplishment—we didn't kill all the plants before they matured! So use up all those beautiful cucumbers in this yummy sour cream dish. It is a great side to any meal. Especially fun at a barbecue. If you like cucumbers in vinegar, well, this dish simply takes it to the next level. You'll crave it!

4 cucumbers (peeled and sliced thinly)
1 small yellow onion (diced)
salt to taste
8oz. (225g) tub sour cream
⅓ cup **Garden Blend Vinegar** (see page 21)
⅓ cup sugar
½ tsp. dried mustard

Place cucumbers and onion in a bowl. Salt very well. Place in refrigerator for 2 to 3 hours. Rinse well and drain. Mix sour cream, vinegar, sugar and mustard together until smooth. Combine this mixture with the cucumbers. Store in refrigerator until it's time to serve. Serves at least 8.

Dilled Carrots

As a child, Dixie thought eating cooked carrots was a form of childhood torture. Not that her mom wasn't a good cook, but cooked carrots were just gross! If you have children that have similar emotional challenges, then this may be the answer. This is a chilled and marinated dish. It is definitely unique and may not be pleasing to everyone. But we think you should try it. And by the way, Dixie now loves carrots—at least the ones prepared this way.

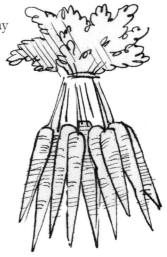

1 tsp. minced garlic
1 Tbs. Dijon mustard
2 Tbs. **Lemon Dill Vinegar** (see page 24)
1 tsp. lemon juice
1 tsp. honey
½ tsp. salt
¼ tsp. freshly ground pepper
3 Tbs. olive oil
4 cups shredded carrots
2 Tbs. fresh chopped dill weed

Mix the garlic, mustard, vinegar, lemon juice, honey, oil, salt and pepper in a blender. Place shredded carrots in a bowl, and gently pour the mixture over the carrots. Add fresh dill and toss. Refrigerate for at least 10 minutes, longer if possible. The longer the carrots marinate, the more tender they will be. Serves 4-6.

Herbed Stuffing

Stuffing…it's not just for Thanksgiving anymore! Or at least that's how we feel about this recipe. For many people, stuffing is a comfort food and, mama, will this one comfort! It is really pretty basic in its ingredients, except for maybe the pine nuts, and they can be optional if you want to leave them out. But pine nuts or not, don't miss trying this one soon. Note: If you are drying your own bread crumbs, be sure to use a good quality bread. It really can make a difference in the flavor of your stuffing.

8 cups dried bread cubes
⅔ cup butter
½ cup onion (chopped)
2 cups celery (finely chopped)
2 tsp. salt
freshly ground pepper
1 tsp. poultry seasoning
1 Tbs. **Garden Blend Vinegar** (see page 21)
1 can water chestnuts (chopped)
½ cup pine nuts
1-2 cups chicken broth

In a large skillet, melt butter; add onion and celery and cook until transparent. Add seasonings, vinegar and bread crumbs. Heat until butter is absorbed. Stir in water chestnuts and pine nuts. Add chicken broth until desired moistness is achieved. Spoon into casserole dish, cover with foil and heat in oven at 325°F (160°C) until hot. Serves 8-10.

Marinated Garden Veggies

Once you serve this recipe, you'll be asked to bring it to parties over and over again, because everyone will love these very scrumptious veggies. Dixie's sister, Wendi, says that broccoli is an especially good veggie to use because the marinade gets in between the little florets and acts like little spoons to scoop up the dressing. A sweet and tangy concoction, you may want to drink the marinade and forget the rest…we're not kidding.

Gather an assortment of fresh vegetables that may include the following:

4 stalks broccoli (cut into small florets)
10 mushrooms
3 stalks celery (sliced into sticks)
1 red, yellow and green bell pepper (sliced into rings)
3 large carrots (sliced into sticks)
2-3 onions (finely chopped)

Marinade:

1 cup sugar
2 tsp. dry mustard
1 tsp. salt
1 Tbs. poppy seeds
½ cup **Garden Blend Vinegar** (see page 21)
½ cup vegetable oil

Blend marinade ingredients together in a blender and set aside. In a container with a tight-fitting lid, prepare veggies in an attractive manner sprinkling chopped onion evenly over the top. Pour marinade over the vegetables, and cover and refrigerate. Best if marinated for 2 to 3 hours before serving. (After an hour, turn veggie container upside down so the tops of the vegetables get marinated as well. When you go to serve it, return to its upright position.) Easily serves 8.

Mushroom Pilaf

Our families love rice and so we are always looking for new and different ways to prepare it. This is a great recipe that you will love. You'll find it is easy to prepare and it will probably become one of your family's favorites. By adding a little chicken or pork, you could serve it as a main dish.

1 cup long grain rice (uncooked)
½ cup onion (chopped)
1lb. (455g) fresh mushrooms (sliced)
½ cup butter
3 cups chicken broth
½ cup **Oriental Spice Vinegar** (see page 24)
2 tsp. salt
⅛ tsp. white pepper
1 cup frozen peas (thawed)
¼ cup fresh grated Parmesan cheese
2 tomatoes diced
14oz. (400g) can artichoke hearts (quartered)

In large skillet, sauté onions, mushrooms in butter for 8 minutes. Add rice and continue cooking for 2 minutes. Add broth, vinegar, artichokes and seasonings. Mix well. Cook in uncovered casserole 45 minutes at 350°F (180°C). When it has cooked for 35 minutes, add chopped tomatoes and peas, stirring gently. Also, stir in half of the Parmesan cheese. Sprinkle remaining cheese on top. Return to oven for the remaining 10 minutes uncovered. Serves 8.

Orange Sherbet Salad

Jello…yes jello. It is amazing what a little vinegar can do to jello! You thought jello jiggled before. Well, wait till you get a taste of this. Great little salad that can be served buffet style or dress it up on individual plates on a bed of shredded lettuce. Either way, this tangy tropical delight will bring life to any meal.

6oz. (170g) package orange jello
1 cup boiling water
1 cup orange juice
3 Tbs. **Tangy Citrus Vinegar** (see page 27)
1 pint tropical flavored sherbet
6oz. (170g) cream cheese
¼ cup orange juice

¼ cup sugar
1 Tbs. grated orange rind
12oz. (340g) cool whip

In a large bowl, dissolve jello in the boiling water. Add orange juice, sherbet and vinegar. Mix until sherbet is melted. Pour into a 9x11-inch (23x28cm) glass casserole dish. Add the mandarin oranges. Chill until set. In a separate bowl, cream together cream cheese, ¼ cup orange juice, sugar, orange rind and cool whip. Beat until well mixed. Spread on set salad. Chill. You may serve this salad from the dish or cut and place on small individual plates on a bed of shredded lettuce. You may also set this salad in a mold. Serves 8-10.

Peas with Walnuts

This is a great side addition to a dinner that is served cold. Maybe with pasta or a tossed salad or even a fruit salad. And we're saying that because this recipe is served chilled. When you are assigned a vegetable dish for an outdoor party or barbecue, try this one. It's deliciously simple. Promise!

2lbs. (900g) frozen baby peas (thawed, chilled)
1 red onion (chopped)
8oz. (225g) walnuts (toasted, chopped)
½lb. (225g) bacon (cooked, crumbled)
½ cup walnut oil
¼ cup **Chive Blossom Vinegar** (see page 19)
2 Tbs. water
1 Tbs. sugar
1 Tbs. fresh chives (chopped)
1 Tbs. Dijon mustard
¼ tsp. freshly ground pepper

Combine peas, red onion, bacon & walnuts in a bowl. Chill. Whisk together oil, vinegar, water, sugar, chives, mustard, and pepper. You may also buzz these ingredients together in a blender. Pour over your pea mixture and chill. Serve. Serving it hot is always an option too. Just heat on low on the stove and serve. Serves 8.

Note: If you don't have Chive Blossom Vinegar on hand, try Farmers Market, Hot Pepper or Provencal instead.

Potato Bake

These are a quick and easy finger food and are a nice side dish for any casual dinner. Maybe they could be considered the healthy version of French fries. And if you really want to create a stir, sprinkle grated cheddar or Parmesan cheese over the top for the last 5 or so minutes in the oven. Wow!

10-12 small red potatoes (washed, not peeled, cut in quarters)
⅓ cup **Lemon Dill Vinegar** (see page 24)
1 cube butter (melted)
1 tsp. dried dill weed
salt and pepper to taste
4 green onions (finely chopped)

In a shallow baking dish (we use a 9x13-inch, 23x33cm, cake pan) arrange the quartered red potatoes in a single layer. Drizzle vinegar over the top. Next, drizzle   butter in same manner. Sprinkle with salt, pepper, dill and onions. Bake uncovered at 350°F (180°C) for 35 to 40 minutes or until tender when speared with a fork. Serves 4-6.

Stuffed Portabella Mushrooms

When we go to a party or a dinner and stuffed mushrooms are on the menu, we acknowledge that the hostess has put a great deal of thought into her menu. There's no doubt about it, you'll have to plan ahead to make this side dish. Unless, of course, you keep portabella mushrooms and shrimp on hand. If you do, then this is a heaven sent recipe to your kitchen. The mushrooms are beautifully impressive, and not hard to create. Serve them with roast beef, pasta salad, or even a fruit salad. Your family or guests will be very impressed with your culinary skills.

¾ cup sour cream
½lb. (225g) small, cooked shrimp
3 green onions (chopped)
1 cup mozzarella cheese (shredded)
1 cup parmesan cheese (shredded)
2 Tbs. **Hot Pepper Vinegar** (see page 23)
1 tsp. fresh parsley (finely chopped)

10 small portabella mushrooms (without stems)
2 fresh cloves garlic (minced)
olive oil
balsamic vinegar
salt and pepper to taste

In a bowl, combine sour cream, shrimp, green onions, Hot Pepper Vinegar, parsley and cheeses. Add salt and pepper to taste. Set aside. In a large skillet, pour equal amounts of olive oil and balsamic vinegar to cover the bottom. Add minced garlic and heat. Place mushrooms in pan and sauté for about 7 minutes, turning over several times. Place all mushrooms on their tops and add ¼ tsp. of balsamic vinegar to the underside of each mushroom. Grease a shallow, glass baking dish and arrange mushrooms top side down. Spoon sour cream mixture onto each mushroom. Bake at 375°F (190°C) for approximately 20 minutes or until hot. Serves 5 or 10, you decide.

Tantalizing Tangy Tomatoes

This is a must try when the summer tomatoes are ripe, the evenings are warm, and the patio is calling for a cook out. A great dish for the light appetite and it's low in fat, too!

What more could you ask for?

½ cup **Garden Blend Vinegar** (see page 21)
¼ cup apple cider vinegar
½ cup cold water
3 tsp. sugar
4 large tomatoes (thinly sliced)
3 green onions (chopped)

Place sliced tomatoes in a shallow serving bowl. Sprinkle green onions over the tomatoes. In a small mixing bowl, combine vinegars, water and sugar, making sure that the sugar is dissolved. Completely cover the tomatoes with the vinegar mixture. Cover and chill for 1 hour before serving. Serves 4-6.

Tartar Sauce

We seem to be hearing a lot in recent years about how good fish is for us. Well, we can't say from a health perspective, but we can assure you that your fish will be fantastic dipped in our incredible tartar sauce. You may like it so much you'll want to use it on other things as well…you know, like the way we use Ranch dressing. It goes with everything!

1½ cups mayonnaise
1 hard-boiled egg (finely chopped)
2 Tbs. fresh parsley (minced)
2 Tbs. capers
1 tsp. fresh chives (minced)
2 tsp. prepared horseradish
1 tsp. fresh lemon juice
1 Tbs. **Farmers Market Vinegar** (see page 20)
1 tsp. Dijon mustard
½ tsp. dried tarragon

Combine all ingredients, stirring well. Store in an airtight container in refrigerator. Makes about 2 cups. Serve with your favorite fish or try our Fried Mushroom recipe (see page 35).

Walnut Spread

Picture this: A bowl of steaming hot soup or chili, preferably one of our recipes, a hot loaf of French baguette bread, and…butter? Come on now! Let's use our imaginations. Wouldn't the whole scene taste better with a wonderful and unique spread for your warm bread. You'll love the heartiness of this recipe. The walnuts give it so much flavor and, of course, the vinegar adds the extra punch it needs to make it taste gourmet. You'll love it!

1 cup canned garbanzo beans (about half of a 15oz. can)
½ cup walnuts (chopped)
½ cup fresh basil leaves (lightly packed)
1 Tbs. olive oil
1 Tbs. **Tangy Citrus Vinegar** (see page 27)
⅛ tsp. salt
⅛ tsp. freshly ground pepper
toasted thin baguette slices

Drain garbanzo beans, reserve liquid. In a blender or food processor, combine beans and 2 tablespoons of the reserved liquid, walnuts, basil leaves, olive oil, vinegar, salt and pepper. Cover and process until nearly smooth. Scrape down sides and add additional reserved liquid if mixture appears too stiff. Serve on toasted slices of bread. Cover and refrigerate up to 5 days. Makes 1¼ cups.

For the Sweet Tooth

inegar in salads and main courses, yes—but desserts, too? You may be saying to yourself, "I don't want to try any of these recipes." Well, let us just say, you'll be making a very big mistake if you don't! We have told you many times before, how vinegar simply enhances the flavors of the ingredients in the recipe. Well, it's no different here. Now, we will shamefully admit that we were a little reluctant at first to add vinegar to ice cream and cake. But we warn you, don't knock it 'til you try it! Our children remember the good ol' days when we threatened to sprinkle vinegar on their cheerios. Now, they love to walk into the kitchen and see us adding vinegar to their favorite recipes, regardless of whether it is a snack, the main course or yes, even dessert!

Of course, when you are experimenting on your own recipes, we would suggest that fruit vinegars are the place to start. The thought of herbal vinegars and chocolate together makes us want to go on a diet! We really believe that these are some of the most delicious dessert recipes on the face of the planet. We hope you enjoy!

Apple Cinnamon Crunch

You will be amazed at what a wonderful difference using our Apple Cinnamon Vinegar makes in this apple dessert. The vinegar brings out all of the different flavors and enhances them so that your taste buds will stand at attention. And believe us, your friends and family will give you plenty of attention if they are treated to this dish from time to time.

8-10 apples of your choice (cored, peeled and sliced thinly)
4 Tbs. **Apple Cinnamon Vinegar** (see page 17)
1½ cups sugar
4 Tbs. flour
3 Tbs. cinnamon
1 cup butter (cold and cut into small pieces)
2 cups quick or old fashioned oats
1 cup brown sugar (packed well)
½ tsp. salt
½ cup flour

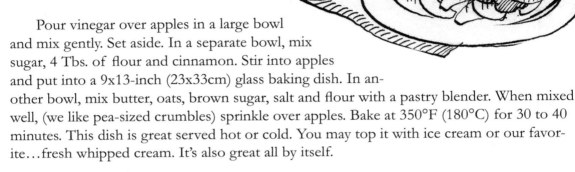

Pour vinegar over apples in a large bowl and mix gently. Set aside. In a separate bowl, mix sugar, 4 Tbs. of flour and cinnamon. Stir into apples and put into a 9x13-inch (23x33cm) glass baking dish. In another bowl, mix butter, oats, brown sugar, salt and flour with a pastry blender. When mixed well, (we like pea-sized crumbles) sprinkle over apples. Bake at 350°F (180°C) for 30 to 40 minutes. This dish is great served hot or cold. You may top it with ice cream or our favorite…fresh whipped cream. It's also great all by itself.

Apple Pumpkin Cake

You know a recipe is a winner when your pickiest daughter requests this cake every year for her birthday! She doesn't want a princess cake from a great bakery, or an ice cream cake from Baskin Robbins, she wants an Apple Pumpkin Cake made by her mom!

How cool is that? The cake is so moist and the cream cheese frosting adds just the right amount of sweetness. You might want to make a little extra frosting—the thicker, the better—you can never have too much!

4 eggs
1½ cups sugar
½ cup vegetable oil
1 cup applesauce
2 cups Libby pumpkin
2 Tbs. **Spice Apple Vinaigrette** (see page 55)
2 cups flour
2 tsp. baking powder
2 tsp. cinnamon
1 tsp. soda

1 tsp. salt
1 tsp. nutmeg
8oz. (225g) cream cheese
½ cup butter (softened to room temperature)
1 tsp. vanilla
3 cups powdered sugar
2-3 tsp. milk

In mixer, blend eggs, sugar, oil, applesauce, pumpkin and vinegar. Slowly add flour, baking powder, cinnamon, soda, salt and nutmeg. Blend until smooth. Place in a greased 9x13-inch (23x33cm) pan and bake for 25 to 30 minutes at 350°F (180°C). Insert toothpick to make sure it is done. While cake is cooling, combine cream cheese, butter, vanilla and sugar in a bowl and mix until creamy. Add the milk to get the desired consistency. Spread over the cooled cake and enjoy.

Berry Crumble

What better way to celebrate a beautiful harvest of berries than to put them all together in a dish you'll want to take to all your parties. Fresh berries are always the best, but this recipe must be used year-round—so it's alright if you must use frozen berries. If there were dessert awards, this would get an Oscar.

½ cup sugar
½ cup flour
2 cups fresh blueberries
2 cups fresh raspberries
1 Tbs. **Tangy Citrus Vinegar** (see page 27)
1 Tbs. **Blueberry Vinegar** (see page 17)
1 cup quick or old fashioned oats (uncooked)
1 cup brown sugar (firmly packed)
1 cup butter (cut into small pieces)
dash of salt

Preheat oven to 350°F (180°C). Combine sugar and flour in a bowl. Gently fold in blueberries, raspberries and vinegars. Spoon into a 8x8 (20x20cm) glass baking dish. In a separate bowl, combine oats and brown sugar and salt. Cut butter into oat mixture until pieces are the size of small peas. Sprinkle over berries. Bake for 40 to 45 minutes or until berries are bubbling around the edges and topping is slightly browned. Serve warm with a scoop of vanilla bean ice cream. It doesn't get any better than this!

Cranberry Sorbet

In Italy, they serve a sorbet between the salad and the main course to cleanse the palate. But here in "vinegar heaven" we say…serve it any time you darn well please!

We're so American, aren't we? Sorbet is not too sweet and is very light. It would be an especially nice dessert after a rich dinner. Looks pretty in tall martini glasses with butter cookies served on the side.

10-12oz. (285-340g) frozen cranberry juice cocktail
1 Tbs. **Cranberry Vinegar** (see page 17)
1 Tbs. low-fat vanilla flavored yogurt
2 large scoops raspberry sherbet
¼ cup frozen blueberries
½ cup frozen strawberries
crushed ice

Combine all ingredients in blender and blend until smooth. The amount of ice you add will determine the thickness. This recipe may be served as a smoothie, frozen into a sorbet or frozen and served with Sprite as a slush. Makes a great, light dessert.

Cran-Orange Muffins

This is a great way to say "Happy Holidays" to your family and friends on cold winter mornings. These muffins would be a great addition to your Christmas brunch. They are both sweet and tart and can be very addicting. A gourmet treat that may become a favorite year round. If so, feel free to substitute frozen cranberries for fresh.

2¼ cups flour
1 cup sugar
1½ tsp. baking powder
1 tsp. salt
½ tsp. baking soda
4 Tbs. cold butter
1 egg (beaten)
grated zest of 1 orange
⅓ cup **Tangy Citrus Vinegar** (see page 27)
4 Tbs. sugar

⅓ cup orange juice
1 Tbs. **Cranberry Cinnamon Vinegar** (see page 19)
2½ cups fresh cranberries
orange flavored sugar crystals

Preheat oven to 350°F (180°C). Grease muffin pan. In a large bowl, mix the flour, 1 cup sugar, baking powder, salt and baking soda. Using a pastry blender, cut the butter into the dry mixture until it is crumbly. Add the egg and orange zest. In a small bowl, mix the vinegars, 4 Tbs. sugar and the orange juice. Add this to the large bowl mixture. Stir by hand just until evenly moistened. Fold in cranberries gently. Spoon batter into muffin tin. Sprinkle sugar crystals on top. Bake for approximately 20 minutes. Makes 1 dozen.

Frozen Strawberry Treat

If you like strawberries, you may want to mark this page with a sticky note. It is delicate and delectable! We crave it almost like we crave our diet coke—a legal addictive stimulant. It is great served as described for large groups. But if you're looking for something very impressive, try layering it in beautiful flute or parfait glasses. You will get rave reviews.

1 cup flour
⅓ cup brown sugar (well packed)
½ cup pecans (chopped)
½ cup melted butter

Mix the above ingredients and spread on a cookie sheet. Bake for 15 minutes at 350°F (180°C), stirring the mixture several times as it bakes. Cool. Crumble ⅔ of this mixture into a 9x13-inch (23x33cm) pan.

2 egg whites
⅔ cup sugar
1 Tbs. fresh lemon juice
2 Tbs. **Strawberry Vinegar** (see **Basic Berry Vinegar**, page 17)
10oz. (285g) package frozen strawberries (thawed and sliced)
1 cup cool whip

Chill a large mixing bowl and beaters. Then, beat the egg whites, strawberries, sugar, lemon juice and vinegar for 10 minutes. Fold in the cool whip. Spread evenly over the crumb mixture that you prepared earlier. Sprinkle with remaining ⅓ crumble mixture. Freeze overnight or at least for 6 hours before serving. Serve frozen, but set out for 10 to 15 minutes before serving. This recipe can be made days ahead! Serves 12.

Fruit Cookie Pizza

This dessert will cause a sensation! It is so beautiful, it actually looks like art. But once you get a taste of this sweet, fruity confection, you'll say to heck with the art—let's dig in! Don't hesitate for even a moment to get your slice, because you know the old adage: you snooze, you lose!

Cookie base:

> 4 eggs
> 1 cup shortening
> 2 cups sugar
> 1 tsp. vanilla
> 1 tsp. baking soda
> 1 tsp. salt
> 4 tsp. baking powder
> 1 cup sour cream
> 5 cups flour

In mixer, beat eggs. Add shortening and sugar until creamed. Add vanilla, baking soda, salt and baking powder. Add flour and sour cream alternately. When well mixed, put bowl of dough in freezer and let chill while you clean up the kitchen (maybe 10 or 15 minutes.) Remove dough from freezer. Roll out enough dough to cover the pizza pan you are going to bake it on. Roll out the dough until it is approximately ¼ inch thick. Carefully roll dough onto your rolling pin and slide gently onto pizza pan. Bake in the oven at 375°F (190°C) for approximately 10 minutes or until edge of cookie starts to turn a light golden color. Cool. (You'll have cookie dough left over, so bake some cookies too.) Bake smaller cookies at 375°F (190°C) for 8 to 10 minutes. Frost if desired.

Cream Cheese filling:

> 8oz. (225g) package cream cheese
> 1 tsp. vanilla
> ½ cup powdered sugar
> fruit of Choice: Select a nice variety of color and size. Some of our favorites are: strawberries, kiwi, bananas, blueberries, mandarin oranges, grapes.

Glaze:

> 1 cup orange juice
> ½ cup lemon juice
> 1¾ cup sugar
> ¼ cup **Tangy Citrus Vinegar** (see page 27)
> ¾ cup water
> 3½ Tbs. cornstarch

While cookie is cooling, mix together the cream cheese filling in a small bowl. When cookie is completely cool, gently spread filling over cookie. Cover with plastic wrap and chill in refrigerator overnight.

In a small saucepan, combine glaze ingredients together and bring to a boil on medium heat. Thicken with cornstarch. Remove from heat and let cool. Place in bowl and store in refrigerator until next day.

Next Day: Remove cookie pizza with cream filling and glaze from refrigerator. Arrange the fruit you have chosen on top of your pizza. Once fruit is in place, spoon enough glaze over the fruit to completely cover. (The glaze will keep the fruit looking fresh.) Cover with foil and return to the refrigerator until ready to serve. It is nice to chill it for at least an hour before serving. Slice with a large knife or pizza cutter when serving.

Lemon Pound Cake

Pound cake is an old fashioned type dessert that we don't see served often enough anymore. When we were young, it was always our old aunts that would unwrap this treasure at family parties. Everyone would rave about the moist, wonderful flavor. So we decided to share this updated version of a wonderful pound cake recipe. All of our aunts would be so proud.

1 cup butter (softened to room temperature)
3 cups sugar
1 Tbs. lemon extract
1 tsp. almond extract
2 Tbs. **Tangy Citrus Vinegar**
(see page 27)
6 eggs
¼ tsp. soda
3 cups flour (unsifted)
1 cup sour cream
4 Tbs. lemon or orange juice
¼ cup sugar

Beat together butter, 3 cups sugar, lemon and almond extract, and vinegar. When well mixed, add eggs one at a time, beating after each. Stir soda into flour and add flour mixture and sour cream alternately to the cream mixture, mixing just until well combined. Spoon batter into well greased and floured 10-inch (25cm) bundt pan or tube pan. Bake at 325°F (160°C) for approximately 1 hour and 15 minutes or until toothpick comes out clean. Cool in pan about 15 minutes, then turn out onto a dinner plate. Mix remaining ¼ cup sugar, and 4 Tbs. juice in a small bowl and drizzle over the warm cake. Allow a few moments for the excess topping to be absorbed into the underside of the cake. Then wrap cake up tightly in plastic wrap. Best if made the day before serving. When ready to eat, unwrap and serve.

Orange Squeeze Cake

When was the last time you received a nice big squeeze? That long, huh? Well, make this cake and you'll have to beat 'em off with a spoon! The aroma that fills the air when this cake is baking is so incredible that you will not have to burn your smelly candles for a week! This is real treat for citrus lovers.

1 large orange
1 cup raisins
⅓ cup walnuts
2 cups flour
1 tsp. baking soda
1 tsp. salt
1 cup sugar
½ cup shortening
1 cup milk
2 eggs
2 Tbs. **Creamsicle Vinegar** (see page 20)

Topping:

⅓ cup reserved orange juice
⅓ cup sugar
1 tsp. cinnamon
¼ cup walnuts (chopped)

Squeeze juice from orange. Set aside for topping. In a food processor, grind together orange pulp and rind, raisins and walnuts. In a separate bowl, sift together flour, soda, salt and sugar. Add shortening to the dry ingredients and mix well. Next, add in milk and eggs. Blend until smooth. Fold in orange/raisin mixture. Pour into a greased 9x13-inch (23x33cm) pan. Bake 40 to 45 minutes at 350°F (180°C). Cool slightly. Drizzle reserved orange juice over top of cake. In a small bowl combine sugar, cinnamon and walnuts. Sprinkle immediately over warm cake. Makes a great brunch cake.

Peaches and Cream

We love this recipe so much that we really must admit that the ice cream is somewhat of an afterthought. We prefer to just ladle some into a cereal bowl and go after it with a nice big spoon. It is the perfect dessert for a warm summer evening when the peaches are ripe.

5 large ripe peaches (peeled and pitted)
¾ cup sugar
¼ cup **Creamsicle Vinegar** (see page 20)

Place 4 of the peaches, sugar and vinegar in the blender and blend well. Add the fifth peach and pulse a couple of times to allow a few chunky pieces of fruit to be visible. Chill well. Pour over individual servings of vanilla bean ice cream. Great as a fruit dip, too.

Note: Could be done using frozen peaches. It won't be quite as tasty, but would work in a pinch.

Pineapple Crunch

Just the thought of fresh pineapple makes our mouths water. The sweetness of ripe pineapple chunks warmed with spices and a crunchy topping, makes us want to cuddle up with a good book, our favorite blanky and dive into a deep bowl of this delectable treat.

6 cups fresh pineapple (diced)
3 Tbs. **Tangy Citrus Vinegar** (see page 27)
2 Tbs. honey
¼ cup sugar
2 Tbs. flour
½ tsp. cinnamon
½ tsp. nutmeg
2 cups shredded coconut
1 cup quick or old fashioned oats
1 cup flour
1 cup brown sugar (firmly packed)
½ tsp. cinnamon
1 cup butter or margarine (softened)

Combine the first seven ingredients in a bowl. Mix well. Pour into a slightly greased 2½-quart (2.5L) casserole dish. In another bowl, combine coconut, oats, flour, brown sugar and cinnamon. Cut butter into dry mixture until it looks like a coarse meal. Sprinkle evenly over the pineapple mixture. Bake at 350°F (180°C) for 20 to 25 minutes. Make sure the pineapple is slightly tender and the top is a golden brown. Serve warm or cold with ice cream or fresh whipped cream. Scrumptious!

Pineapple Sherbet

This is a nice little dessert that grandmas love. Very easy to make and stick in the freezer. Looks very pretty in a big glass punch bowl mixed with Sprite as a slush. Better yet, surprise the one you love by serving it in a fancy champagne glass for a special occasion. Did you know that pineapple is a natural aphrodisiac? Just kiddin'!

1¾ cup milk (not skim)
¼ cup **Creamsicle Vinegar** (see page 20)
8oz. (225g) can crushed pineapple (do not drain)
¾ cup sugar

Place milk in a large bowl and add vinegar. Let stand for 5 minutes. Add the pineapple with the juice and sugar. Mix together with a spoon until sugar is dissolved. Freeze in an air-tight container or zip-lock bag until frozen. Makes approximately 3 cups.

Note: You can vary this recipe by adding other types of fruit such as bananas, mandarin oranges, raspberries, etc. You could also serve it with Sprite as a slush.

Pumpkin Cake Roll

It is hard to beat the flavors of pumpkin and cream cheese icing all rolled together in one delectable dessert. We used to think of pumpkin in the context of cool, crisp autumn afternoons. But this recipe may rewrite dessert history as you have known it. If you really want to create a stir, serve it as part of your Easter buffet or your 4th of July picnic!

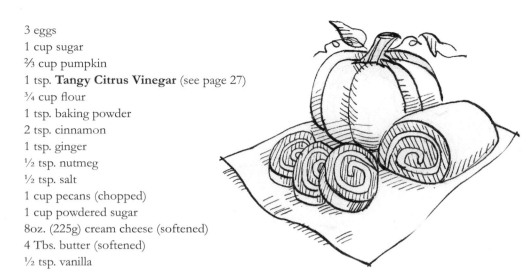

3 eggs
1 cup sugar
⅔ cup pumpkin
1 tsp. **Tangy Citrus Vinegar** (see page 27)
¾ cup flour
1 tsp. baking powder
2 tsp. cinnamon
1 tsp. ginger
½ tsp. nutmeg
½ tsp. salt
1 cup pecans (chopped)
1 cup powdered sugar
8oz. (225g) cream cheese (softened)
4 Tbs. butter (softened)
½ tsp. vanilla

Beat eggs in mixer for 5 minutes. Gradually beat in sugar. Fold in pumpkin, vinegar, flour, baking powder, cinnamon, ginger, nutmeg and salt. Spread onto a greased and floured jelly roll pan. Sprinkle with nuts. Bake for 15 minutes at 350°F (180°C). Immediately turn out onto a dish towel that has been sprinkled with powdered sugar. While still hot, roll cake and towel into a long roll and place on cooling rack to cool. In a small mixing bowl, beat powdered sugar, cream cheese, butter and vanilla together to make the filling. When cake is cool, unroll and spread filling evenly on cake. Re-roll without the towel, cover with plastic wrap and   refrigerate until ready to serve. Slice the thickness you prefer.

Note: A warm caramel sauce would be heavenly drizzled over the cold cake…just food for thought!

Red Velvet Cake

This cake is delicious to the taste, but even more than that, it is absolutely beautiful. The deep red of the cake layers, separated by the creamy white icing really catches the eye and makes you want burst into verses of the National Anthem. This could also be a sweet little tradition to enjoy on Valentines Day.

1 cup butter
1½ cups sugar
2 eggs
2 Tbs. cocoa
1 tsp. vanilla
1 cup buttermilk
2½ cups flour
1½ tsp. soda
1 Tbs. **Raspberry Vinegar** (see page 17)
2oz. (58g) red food coloring (2 small bottles)
½ tsp. salt

Cream butter, sugar and eggs. In another bowl, make a paste with the cocoa and food coloring. Add to the butter mixture. In another bowl, mix salt and vanilla with buttermilk, soda and vinegar. Add alternately with flour to cream mixture. Stir until mixed well. Pour into two round cake pans, greased and floured. Bake at 350°F (180°C) for approximately 30 minutes or until toothpick comes out clean. When completely cool, slice each cake in half. This will give you four layers for your cake. Place first layer on serving dish, spread a layer of white frosting, add another cake layer and continue this process until all 4 layers have been frosted.

Frosting:

4 Tbs. flour
1 cup milk
½ cup butter
½ cup shortening
1 cup sugar
2 tsp. vanilla
dash of salt

In a saucepan, cook flour and milk over medium heat until thick. Cool. In a separate bowl, cream together butter, sugar and shortening. Add milk mixture, vanilla and salt. Whip together until fluffy. Now you are ready to frost the cake.

Spiced Chocolate Sheet Cake

Chocolate lovers will come running when they smell this cake baking. It simply melts in your mouth. The thin style of the cake is perfect because it allows the chocoholic to have more frosting with each and every bite. Be careful if left alone in the house with this cake. It will call to you…and you will answer with a big fork.

1 cup butter
1 cup water
4 Tbs. cocoa
2 cups flour
2 cups sugar
½ tsp. salt
1 tsp. cinnamon
2 eggs (beaten)
1 tsp. soda
½ cup buttermilk
2 Tbs. **Apple Cinnamon Vinegar** (see page 17)
1 tsp. vanilla

In a small saucepan, bring butter, water and cocoa to a boil over medium heat, stirring constantly. Cool. In a separate bowl, combine flour, sugar, salt, soda and cinnamon. To cooled cocoa mixture, add beaten eggs, vinegar, buttermilk and vanilla. Mix well. Add to dry ingredients. Blend together until smooth. Pour into a greased jelly roll pan and bake at 350°F (180°C) for 20 to 25 minutes or until tooth pick inserted comes out clean.

Prepare the frosting while cake is baking as it is important to frost the cake while it is warm.

Frosting:

3 Tbs. cocoa
6 Tbs. evaporated milk
½ cup butter
1lb. (455g) powdered sugar
½ tsp. vanilla

In a small saucepan, melt butter over medium heat. Add milk and cocoa. Heat, but do not boil. Pour hot mixture into a bowl and add powdered sugar and vanilla. Beat until creamy. Immediately pour over warm cake and spread evenly.

Vinegar Pie Crust

When we say you can use vinegar in anything, we really mean it! This is a terrific, basic piecrust recipe. It is light and flakey and has a wonderful flavor. It was shared with us several years ago by a friend who is well known for her wonderful homemade pies. You can vary the type of vinegar called for in the recipe depending on what type of filling you are going to be using: i.e., strawberry vinegar with strawberry pie.

4 cups flour
1¾ cups shortening
1 Tbs. sugar
1 tsp. salt
1 egg
1 Tbs. **Tangy Citrus Vinegar** (see page 27)
½ cup ice water

Cut together flour, shortening, sugar and salt with pastry blender or fork until pea sized. In a separate bowl, mix together egg, vinegar and water. Sprinkle egg mixture over flour mixture and mix lightly with fork. Knead 7 to 8 times to form a ball. Do not over-knead. This will create a tough piecrust. Cut ball into four parts. Wrap tightly in plastic wrap and chill for 2 to 3 hours before rolling out. When ready to use, roll out and shape in pie dish. Bake at 350°F (180°C) for 8 to 12 minutes or until lightly golden. Cool and fill with desired filling.

This recipe makes 4 single or 2 double piecrusts.

Note: The dough may be frozen for 2 to 3 weeks. When ready to use, simply remove from the freezer and let thaw approximately 1 hour before using.

Vinegar Taffy

Tami remembers way back in the olden days when her mom used to make her dates pull this taffy—to keep them out of trouble, if you know what we mean. It's not every candy recipe that calls for vinegar, but this old-fashioned taffy recipe is really great. Can be a fun family activity too.

2 Tbs. butter (plus a little more to grease the pan)
2 cups sugar
½ cup **Berry Vinegar** or **Apple Cinnamon Vinegar** (see page 17)

Grease large pan or cookie sheet. In a saucepan, melt the 2 Tbs. of butter. Add the sugar and vinegar. Stir over medium heat until the sugar is dissolved, then turn up the heat and boil gently, stirring frequently until the mixture reaches 275°F (135°C). Pour into greased cookie sheet and let cool just until you can handle it. Then start the pulling. As it is stretched and pulled, you will notice that

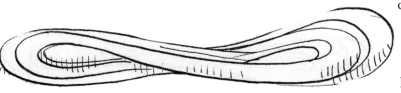

the taffy will become whiter and pearly in color.

If you want the taffy to be colored, add food coloring to the pan when it is cooking. When the taffy gets to the desired consistency, pull into long ropes, twist, and cut into 1-inch pieces with kitchen scissors. Store in an airtight container or wrap individually with wax paper.

The Little Treasure

(Vinegar and Its Many Uses)

Have you ever had an inexpensive maybe even cheap item in your closet or drawer that has been hanging around the house for months, maybe even years, and you have had no use for it? You may have even thought of throwing it out or giving it away. And then one day—in a moment of sheer genius—you discover that this once worthless item has a simple yet miraculous usefulness? It may even become a valued gem. Well folks…let me introduce you to vinegar.

In the other chapters of this book we talk about the wonders of cooking with vinegar. But here, in this one chapter, we are revealing the marvelous wonders of this little treasure. Taken for granted—even verbally abused—this inexpensive yet priceless gem gives and gives in ways that go far beyond human comprehension. After browsing the list below, you will wonder how you have survived to this point in your life without a gallon of vinegar as your constant companion. We hope that the following ideas make life a little easier on you and your pocket book.

Bathroom

- Prevent mold and mildew in the shower. Wipe down tile or formica shower walls with a sponge or cloth dampened with water and vinegar. The vinegar will clean the walls and inhibit the growth of mold and mildew.

- Unclog the showerhead. Mineral deposits from hard water can cause a sputtering, clogged showerhead. Place the showerhead in a pot, add enough vinegar to cover it completely. Heat the vinegar to just below boiling then remove from heat. Leave all to sit for at least six hours. The acid in the vinegar will eat away the deposits. Rinse the showerhead well, and it's ready to go again.

- Combine two tablespoons each of vinegar and baking soda for an effective and inexpensive scouring powder.

- Clean the toilet rim. Put 5% vinegar in a squirt bottle and use it to clean the rim of the toilet. It disinfects, too!

- Clean bathroom and kitchen faucets. Soak a paper towel in vinegar then wrap it around your faucet to remove mineral deposits.

- Clean the build-up and residue on your curling iron with a paste of one part salt and one part vinegar. Rub on barrel of curling iron and wipe off with clean cloth.

Beauty

- For a great pedicure, soak your feet in ½ cup vinegar to 6 cups warm water. Will soften skin. Can also be used for rough elbows.

- Rinse your hair with ½ cup vinegar and two cups warm water after shampooing to eliminate dandruff.

- Remove residue and styling product build-up from hair. After shampooing, rinse your hair with a mixture of equal parts of vinegar and warm water to remove all the build up and get rid of the dullness.

- To eliminate toe fungus, soak feet in a solution of one part vinegar to one part water. Performed regularly, this can clear up the problem. This same remedy can clear up athlete's foot.

- Vinegar can reduce swelling. Try rubbing vinegar on varicose veins to relieve the pain and reduce the swelling.

- Mix equal parts of onion juice and vinegar and apply to age spots. Use daily and within a couple of weeks, age spots will become less noticeable.

- Nail polish will go on smoother and stay on longer if you wipe your nails with white vinegar before applying polish.

- Soak dentures in vinegar rather than denture solution. Brush like normal. Dentures will be whiter and odor free.

- Include vinegar in your diet; it helps prevent fat from accumulating in the body.

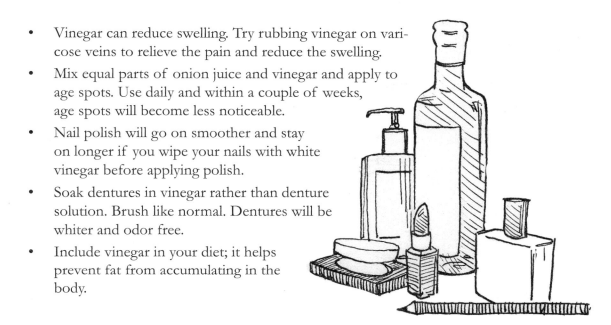

Cleaning

- Spray vinegar around doors, windows, appliances or wherever you have a problem with ants.

- Add a cup of vinegar to dish water when washing glassware and china. Rinse and dry with towel.

- Clean fireplace bricks.

- Clean up cola spills. Using a dry cloth, press on spill to absorb any excess cola. With a clean cloth doused with cool vinegar, dab at the stain until gone. (Never use a hot cloth as it will set the stain in carpet.)

- Eliminate smelly kitchen drains by pouring a cup of vinegar down the drain. Let it stand for 30 minutes and then rinse with water.

- Disinfect wood cutting boards with full strength vinegar.

- Clean the refrigerator with a solution of equal parts of vinegar and water.

- Clean and deodorize your floors. Pour some drops of liquid dishwashing soap in a pail of warm water and add one cup of vinegar. Floors will sparkle.

- Clean woodwork with a mixture of 1 cup ammonia, ½ cup vinegar, ¼ cup baking soda and 1 cup warm water.

- Bathtub film can be removed by wiping with white distilled vinegar and then with soda. Rinse clean with water.

- Stubborn stains can be removed from the toilet by spraying them with white distilled vinegar and brushing vigorously. The bowl may be deodorized by adding 3 cups of white distilled vinegar. Allow it to remain for a half hour, then flush.

- To eliminate mildew, dust and odors, wipe down walls with vinegar-soaked cloth.

- Pour boiling vinegar down clogged drains to unclog and clean them.

- Wipe the inside of the oven frequently with vinegar to prevent grease build-up.

- Clean smelly jars with vinegar and water to remove odor.

- Freshen a lunchbox by soaking a piece of bread in vinegar and let it sit in the lunchbox overnight.

- Clean and deodorize garbage disposals by making vinegar ice cubes and feeding them down the disposal. After grinding, run cold water through.

- Clean the dishwasher. Run a cup of vinegar through the whole cycle once a month to reduce soap build-up on the inner mechanisms and on glassware.

- Wipe stainless steel with a vinegar-dampened cloth for a beautiful shine.

- Remove chewing gum from clothing or rugs by pouring warm vinegar on spot and let it soak.

- Brass, copper and pewter will shine if wiped with a mixture of 1 tsp. salt and 1 cup of distilled vinegar.

- Mix vinegar with linseed oil to clean your wood.

- Clean microwave. Boil a solution of ¼ cup of vinegar and 1 cup of water in the microwave. Will loosen baked-on food and deodorize.

- Clean eyeglasses. Wipe each lens with a drop of vinegar.

- Wipe vent hood over cook top with a soft cloth dampened with vinegar. It will cut through grease and leave stainless steel clean and shiny.

- Clean windows with a mixture of vinegar and water. You can wipe with newspaper or paper towels, whichever you prefer.

Cooking

- Tenderize meat by marinating it overnight in vinegar.

- Add a spoonful of vinegar to cooking water to make cauliflower white and clean.

- When boiling eggs, add some vinegar to the water to prevent white from leaking out of small cracks.

- Add a teaspoon of vinegar to water when poaching eggs to prevent separation.

- Add a spoonful of vinegar when cooking fruit to improve the flavor.
- Add a spoonful of vinegar to boiling ham to improve the flavor and cut the salty taste.
- Add 1 teaspoon vinegar to cooking water for fluffier rice.
- Add vinegar to your deep fryer to eliminate a greasy taste.
- Remove berry stains from hands with vinegar. This also works for Kool-Aid-stained fingers.
- Beat 3 egg whites with a teaspoon of vinegar for fluffier meringue.
- Prevent sugaring by mixing a drop of vinegar into cake icing.
- Adding a few drops of vinegar to water when peeling potatoes will prevent discoloration. They will stay fresh for days in the refrigerator.

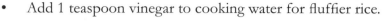

- Make buttermilk by adding a tablespoon of vinegar to a cup of milk and let it stand for 5 minutes to thicken.
- Soak wilted vegetables in a quart of cold water with a tablespoon of vinegar to freshen them up.
- Scale fish more easily. Rub fish with vinegar 5 minutes before scaling.
- Eliminate onion odor. Rub vinegar on your fingers before and after handling onions.
- Wipe jars of preserves and canned food with a vinegar-dampened cloth to prevent mold-producing bacteria.
- Avoid cabbage odor by adding a little vinegar to cooking water.
- No more sticky pasta. Add a couple of drops to your pasta as it boils and it will greatly reduce the starch.

Garden

- Apply full strength to kill grass and weeds on walks and driveways.
- Spray full strength on tops of weeds. Reapply on any new growth until plants have starved.
- In hard water areas, add a cup of vinegar to a gallon of tap water for watering acid-loving plants like rhododendrons, gardenias, or azaleas. The vinegar will release iron

in the soil for the plants to use.

- Keep cut flowers fresh. Add 2 tablespoons vinegar and 1 teaspoon sugar for each quart of water.

- Neutralize garden lime. Rinse your hands liberally with vinegar after working with garden lime to avoid rough and flaking skin. Clean pots before repotting, rinse with vinegar to remove excess lime.

- Keep car windows frost-free. Coat the windows the night before with a solution of three parts vinegar to one part water.

- Soak new propane lantern wicks in vinegar for several hours. Let dry before using. Will burn longer and brighter.

- Clean milking equipment. Rinse with vinegar to leave system clean, odorless, and bacteria free without harmful chemical residue.

Health

- Gently rub cold white vinegar on a sunburn right away for fast relief. It may need to be applied several times.

- Get rid of hiccups quickly by swallowing 1 teaspoon of vinegar.

- Rub skin burns immediately with cold vinegar. It can help prevent blistering.

- Apply vinegar to a bee or jellyfish sting to sooth the itch and sting.

- A couple of tablespoons in bath water will help with dry and itchy skin.

- Soothe a sore throat. Put a teaspoon of vinegar in a glass of water. Gargle, then swallow. For another great gargle, combine 1 c. hot water, 2 tbsp. honey, 1 tbsp. vinegar. Gargle then drink.

- Add a quarter cup of vinegar to the water in a vaporizer to help with chest colds and sinus infections.

- Add 2 spoonfuls of apple cider vinegar and honey in a glass of water daily to help with arthritis.

- Douche with 2-4oz. (58-115g) of vinegar in 2 quarts (2L) of warm water.

- Clear up warts. Apply a lotion of half cider vinegar and half glycerin.

- To soothe headaches, soak a washcloth in cool vinegar and place on your forehead for fast and effective relief.

- To help with reoccurring yeast infections, add 1 cup of vinegar to bath water twice a day. Is also safe to use with children who have yeast infection problems.

- Relieve muscle cramps by rubbing 1 teaspoon of vinegar to the problem muscle.

Laundry

- Add vinegar to laundry rinse water to remove all soap and prevent yellowing.

- Keep colors from running. Immerse clothes in full strength vinegar before washing.

- Remove fabric scorch stains. Lightly rub white distilled vinegar on fabric that has been slightly scorched. Wipe with a clean cloth.

- Freshen up washing machine. Periodically, pour a cup of vinegar in the machine and let it run through a regular cycle (no clothes added). Will dissolve soap residue.

- Brighten fabric colors. Add a ½ cup of vinegar to rinse cycle.

- Take grease off suede. Dip a toothbrush in vinegar and gently brush over grease spot.

- Gently rub vinegar on fabric with tough stains such as fruit, jam, mustard, coffee and tea. Then wash as usual.

- Keep baby clothes smelling fresh by adding 1 cup of vinegar to rinse cycle.

- To get rid of lint and pet hair on clothes, add ½ cup of vinegar to rinse cycle.

- To remove ketchup stains on clothing, treat with a solution of one part vinegar to one part water. Wash normally. This should remove all signs of ketchup.

- Remove perspiration stains. Treat stained area with undiluted vinegar and let sit for an hour or so. Wash as usual.

- After a hem or seam is removed, there are often unsightly holes left in the fabric.

These holes can be removed by placing a cloth, moistened with white distilled vinegar, under the fabric and ironing.

- Remove red clay stains. Make a paste of table salt and vinegar and rub all over the stain. Let sit for 30 minutes. Launder as usual.

- Remove stains from scorched iron plates. Heat equal parts of salt and vinegar in a pan. Rub hot mixture on cool iron plate to remove stain. Clean with soft cloth.

- Add ⅓ cup white vinegar to rinse cycle of whites to keep them beautifully white.

- To add a permanent crease when ironing, mix ⅓ cup vinegar with ⅔ cups water and spray on item you wish to crease. Then place brown paper over fabric and press with a hot iron. This will place a permanent crease in the fabric.

For your Pets

- To get rid of skunk odor from your dog, rub fur with full strength vinegar and rinse.

- Add a tablespoon to pet's drinking water to eliminate odor and encourage shiny fur.

- Keep cats away. Sprinkle vinegar on an area to discourage cats from walking, sleeping or scratching on it.

- Clean the inside of dogs ears with a soft cloth dipped in diluted vinegar to keep the dog from scratching.

- Add a little vinegar to pet's drinking water to keep away fleas and mange. This will also help to stop the tear duct staining some dogs get under their eyes.

- Keep chickens from pecking each other by adding a little cider vinegar to their drinking water.

- Clean up pet urine. Test the color fastness of the carpet first with white distilled vinegar in an inconspicuous place. Then sprinkle distilled vinegar over the fresh pet accident. Wait a few minutes and sponge from the center outward. Blot up with a dry cloth. This procedure may need to be repeated for stubborn stains.

- Add a little vinegar to poultry drinking water to increase egg production and to produce tender meat.

- Clean your aquarium. When the water evaporates, it can leave white mineral deposits at the top of the tank. Simply pour vinegar onto a cloth and wipe away the mineral deposits. It will not hurt the fish and will clean the deposits beautifully.

- Use a mixture of water and vinegar to clean your goldfish bowl. It will help remove any algae growth and will get rid of the odor.

Miscellaneous

- Shine and polish your car chrome with vinegar and a soft cloth.
- Sponge sagging cane chairs with a hot solution of half vinegar and half water. Set in the hot sun to dry.
- Add ½ teaspoon of vinegar per quart of patching plaster to slow the drying process. This will allow more time to work with the area if needed.
- Clean hardened paintbrushes. Simmer in boiling vinegar and wash in hot soapy water.
- Reduce mineral deposits in pipes, radiators, kettles and tanks by adding vinegar into the system.
- Paint adheres better to galvanized metal that has been wiped with vinegar.
- Dissolve rust from bolts and other metals. Soak in full strength vinegar.
- Remove decals by brushing with a couple coats of vinegar. Allow to soak in. Wash off.
- Clean barbeque grill. After grill has cooled enough to clean, spray with straight vinegar to cut through grease and the cooked-on food particles. Use a wire brush to loosen, then rinse. This method is also good on indoor range-top grills.

Just for Kids

Colored Easter Eggs

Mix 1 teaspoon of vinegar with each ½ cup of hot water, then add food coloring. (Check egg-coloring booklets or food dye box for specific directions.) Vinegar keeps the food dyes bright and prevents streaky, uneven colors.

Naked Eggs

Place eggs in a container so the eggs are not touching. Add enough vinegar to cover the eggs. Cover the container, put in the refrigerator and let the eggs sit in the vinegar for 24 hours. Use a large spoon to scoop the eggs out of the container. Be careful since the eggshell has been dissolving, the egg membrane may be the only thing holding the egg together. Carefully dump out the vinegar. Put the eggs back in the container and cover them with fresh vinegar. Leave the eggs in the refrigerator for another 24 hours. Scoop the eggs out again and rinse them carefully. If any of the membranes have broken, throw those eggs away. When you're done, you'll have an egg without a shell.

Dancing Mothballs

Mix 1 cup white vinegar and 2 cups water, green or blue food coloring as desired. In a tall glass bowl or large jar, place several mothballs and add 1 teaspoon baking soda. Pour vinegar mixture over and watch the mothballs dance.

Erupting Volcanoes

First, make the "cone" of the volcano. Mix 6 cups flour, 2 cups salt, 4 tablespoons cooking oil and 2 cups of water. The resulting mixture should be smooth and firm (more water may be added if needed). Stand a soda bottle in a baking pan and mold the dough around it into a volcano shape. Do not cover the hole or drop dough into it. Fill the bottle most of the way full with warm water and a bit of red food coloring (can be done before sculpting if you do not take so long that the water gets cold). Add 6 drops of detergent to the bottle contents. Add 2 tablespoons baking soda to the liquid. Slowly pour vinegar into the bottle. Watch out—eruption time!

Rubber Chicken Legs

Soak chicken bones in vinegar for about five days, and the bones should appear to turn to rubber.

Popping Potion

Materials:

    1 cup water
    3 tsp. baking soda
    2 cup vinegar
    popcorn kernels

Steps:

1. Place a glass on a dish large enough to catch any overflow.

2. Add the soda to the water and stir until it is dissolved.

3. Stir in the vinegar. The mixture should bubble up and spill over the glass.

4. Stir in a spoonful or two of unpopped corn kernels. As they are enveloped by the bubbles, they will rise to the surface.

Index

Notes: